Outside it's War

Janny van der Molen

Outside it's War

Anne Frank and her world

Illustrated by Martijn van der Linden

Ploegsma Publishing House, Amsterdam

www.jannyvandermolen.nl
www.martijnvanderlinden.eu
www.ploegsma.nl
www.annefrank.org

This book was developed in close collaboration with the Anne Frank
House, Amsterdam.
The Dutch Foundation for Literature has contributed to this work by
awarding the author a travel scholarship.

ISBN 978 90 216 7245 8
Copyright © Janny van der Molen 2013
The moral rights of the author have been asserted
Illustrations: Martijn van der Linden 2013, Copyright © Anne Frank House
Copyright © Frank family photographs: Anne Frank House, Amsterdam/
ANNE FRANK-Fonds, Basel
The illustration on page 17 is inspired by a photo of AKG-Images,
Berlin/Hans Asemissen
The illustrations on pages 25 and 45 are inspired by photos of Imagebank
WWII/ The NIOD Institute for War, Holocaust and Genocide Studies,
Amsterdam
Illustration cross-section Anne Frank House: Vizualism (Chantal van
Wessel, Frédérik Ruys)
Translation: Eugenie Martens / Orla Clancy for nltranslations.com
Design: Steef Liefting
First published in Dutch by Ploegsma Publishing House, Amsterdam 2013

Content

Play

6 On June 12th 1929, a little girl was born in the German town of Frankfurt am Main: Annelies Marie Frank. They called her Anne. Anne was the second daughter of Otto and Edith Frank. Her sister's name was Margot. Both Anne's parents came from well-to-do families. Her father worked at the bank owned by his family.

Otto Frank was proud of his country. So much so that he had fought in the German army during World War I (1914-1918). But as Anne grew older, his feelings changed. Germany had huge problems, and was struggling with high unemployment and poverty. At that time, one politician blamed Jewish people for these problems. This politician's name was Adolf Hitler. He advocated a large and powerful Germany. More and more people agreed with him. When elections came they voted for his party. Hitler's followers were called Nazis.

Anne's parents were both Jewish. Her mother went to the synagogue regularly, but her father did not. They both felt comfortable with people who had different beliefs or were not at all religious. It was hard to comprehend that

Anne was four when the family came to live in Amsterdam. It didn't take her long to enjoy her new environment.

they were now seen as the enemy just because they were Jewish.

In 1933, when Adolf Hitler, with the support of many Germans, became leader of the government, Anne's parents decided to move to The Netherlands. They no longer wanted to live in a country where they were hated because of their Jewish roots. Another reason was that the family bank was not doing well.

Anne was four when the family came to live in Amsterdam. It didn't take her long to enjoy her new environment. They had a nice apartment in a neighbourhood where many Jewish families, who had also fled Germany, lived. Anne and Margot quickly learned to speak Dutch and it wasn't long before they felt properly Dutch.

A happy life

'I will never be able to do it!' Her face flushed, Anne was trying hard to keep the hoop rolling. 'It keeps falling down.' Dispirited, she looked at her friend Sanne who managed to keep her hoop rolling beautifully all along the pavement. 'How do you do that?'

'Just set it up straight and give it a big twirl.'

Anne picked up the hoop and followed Sanne's instructions. Yes! It rolled over the pavement, only... to collapse again a few seconds later.

'Well, I'm fed up,' Anne muttered. 'I'd rather ride the scooter.'

Merwede Square, where Anne lived, was a good place to play. Mother kept a watchful eye from the window of their apartment, but knew the girls would be quite safe. As it was not a thoroughfare street, only people who lived on the square cycled or drove their cars there. The pavement and the road were fairly empty. The area was also on the edge of the city. Walk much further, and you would find yourself in fields with cows. The neighbourhood was still very much a construction site. Not far from Anne's apartment block was a large sandy plain where she spent hours playing. Thus Anne grew up in a wonderful home, in a nice street with lovely friends and a great school nearby.

'Peep-peep.'

It was just another normal weekday on Merwede Square, early and even still a bit dark outside. Mother walked to the bedroom Anne and Margot shared.

'Anne, Hannah is waiting downstairs. I can hear her whistle,' she said. Time to walk to school, Anne knew. She put down the book she had been reading, grabbed her coat from the stand, hurried to get it on and was ready to go. 'Wait a minute,' Mother sounded stern. 'It is winter, you will have to wear your *Mütze*.'

'Hat, Mother. The word is 'hat', not *Mütze*. It is not that cold anyway,' Anne muttered. She was eight and felt perfectly capable of deciding for herself whether or not it was necessary to wear a hat.

'You're not leaving the house without it,' Mother said, and Anne knew from her mother's face that it would just be better to obey. She then rushed down the stairs. Mother shouted: 'Take it easy, it could be slippery outside!' But Anne was no longer paying attention. She was in a hurry. She had news for her friend Hannah, whom she always called Hanneli, and she couldn't wait to share it.

'Hanneli, Hanneli! I'm going on a trip. With Father! Just the two of us. Isn't that great? We are going to Switzerland, to Grandma Frank in Basel. Aunt Leni and Uncle Erich live there too, with my cousins Bernd and Stephan, of course. Omi, I always call Grandma 'Omi', has her birthday, as has Stephan and...'

Hannah had to laugh. 'What?' Anne asked in surprise.

'You are talking so fast, it is hard to keep up.'

'Oh, but I'm so excited! Bernd is brilliant at ice-skating, you know, and Omi can tell the greatest stories and...'

'I'm very happy for you, Anne. Really! When are you going?'

'In a few weeks' time. I can hardly wait,' she exclaimed happily.

'Look,' she continued and pointed ahead. 'There are Kitty and Ietje. Shall we give them a good fright?'

Hannah had to laugh. Anne just loved playing tricks on people.

Anne put a finger to her lips and sneaked up on both girls. When she was near enough she poked a finger in their sides and let out a loud 'Boo!'

'Oooh!' Kitty yelled, and Ietje even jumped in fright. Anne collapsed laughing. 'You're a real nuisance!' Kitty said, but she couldn't help but grin.

A few weeks later the day came for Anne and her father to leave on their trip. They took the train to Basel. 'Are we there yet?' Anne kept asking. She knew the answer of course, because only fifteen minutes previously Father had told her they were not even halfway yet. Phew. It was a long way away, Switzerland.

Once they arrived, the long train journey was soon forgotten and she enjoyed playing with Bernd. She had to get used to speaking German again with the family, as it was something they hardly ever did at home anymore. Father and Mother tried to speak as much Dutch as possible.

'I know a fun thing to do,' she whispered in Bernd's ear one afternoon. Bernd and Anne, Aunt Leni, Uncle Erich and Anne's father were visiting Grandma Frank. 'Let's sneak into Omi's bedroom and then you dress up in her clothes.'

Bernd looked at her mischievously. 'And then what?'

'Then you'll pretend to be Omi.'

Bernd grinned. He liked the plan. Together they snuck into the bedroom and Bernd found himself a pretty dress to wear. Anne was choking with laughter. 'A hat!' she said. 'Surely it has a hat to match!' And so Bernd started to rummage for a hat. Then shoes needed to be added. 'The highest heels you can find,' Anne giggled. Bernd grabbed a pair of black high heels. 'Yes, those!'

Bernd proceeded to stride through the room, pretending to be Grandma. Back straight, chin up, nose in the air and

pulling a very proud face. Just like Grandma. It was very funny indeed. Bernd was really good at it! 'You should become an actor!' Anne laughed and Bernd bowed deeply at his enthusiastic audience. 'Thank you, ma'am, thank you!'

Their stay was wonderful, but over far too soon. They had to go home. Father had to go back to work and Anne had to return to school. At home, she looked at a photograph of Bernd. 'I'll be back, Bernd, for sure!' she whispered to the picture. 'After all, you still have to teach me how to ice-skate!'

Thankfully though there were also nice boys to play with at school. 'Last one at the top of the stairs is a loser!' Anne started running at Blankevoort bookshop and turned the corner to Merwede Square. Two boys chased her. 'You're not going to win!' one of them shouted. The other ran as fast as he could, but could not keep up with Anne and his friend Appy.

'I've won!' Appy gasped.

'I'm second,' Anne panted.

'Alright,' Sally said. 'You guys win.'

'I have to catch my breath for a minute,' Anne said, sitting down on the top step of the stone stairs to their first floor apartment. 'Mother doesn't want me to run.'

'Because of your heart?' Sally asked. He looked at Anne with a friendly smile. He had messy blond hair and his chubby cheeks had turned rosy. That was one of the things Anne liked so much about him: his rosy cheeks.

'It's not that bad. Mother just worries a bit too much.'

'But last week you were not at school for a few days because you were sick,' Appy said.

'Just a minor cold,' Anne answered. A challenging look

appeared on her face. 'I may not be strong, but I am certainly pretty!' The boys laughed. That was Anne! Never lost for words!

Anne jumped up, pulled up her socks and straightened her skirt. Mother would have no reason to complain now. Mother liked things neat and orderly. She looked the part now. A neat nine-year old.

'Come on,' she said and rang the doorbell.

Mother opened the door. 'Well, Anne, there you are. Hello Appy. Hello Sally.'

'We're planning to play Monopoly, Mum, if that is okay?'

'Yes, that's fine. How was school?'

'Oh, the usual, Mrs Frank,' Sally answered politely.

The three of them sat at the table and Anne prepared the game, setting out the board, the money, the houses and the pawns.

'Looks difficult,' Appy sighed and he gave Sally an uncertain look.

'Don't worry,' Anne said, 'I'll explain.'

Mother put a plate of biscuits on the table. 'And for each one of you a glass of *Milch*,' she said.

'Milk, Mum,' Anne said. 'Not *Milch*, but 'milk'.' She rolled her eyes and looked at her friends as if to say: that mother of mine will never learn... but Mother just ignored her and returned to the kitchen.

'Look,' Anne said to Appy and Sally. 'You throw the dice and you move forward with your counter. You might end up on a street. All those coloured squares with names represent streets.'

'Trafa... Tra-fal-gar sq-ua-re???' Sally read out aloud. 'What's that?'

'That's English, dummy. These are all streets and squares in London. This is a board game from England.'

'This one's easy,' Appy pointed out. 'This street is called *Strand*.'

'Pronouncing these English words isn't easy,' Anne said, picking up the dice.

'It sure isn't,' Sally muttered. Soon they were so engrossed in the game they forgot all about their milk and biscuits.

Time passed. It was 1938 and five years since the Frank family had moved to Amsterdam. Their life was as normal as any family during that time. Father left in the morning to go to the office and Margot and Anne went to school. Mother cleaned the house, did the shopping and made sure the clothes were washed and neatly folded in the wardrobes. Whenever possible she took the girls out, to the shops, a museum, the cinema or even sometimes on a daytrip to the beach. Margot, who was three years older than Anne, often invited friends over and Anne enjoyed playing with other children.

Father worked long days. Busy as he was, he sometimes had to spend Sundays at the office too, just to catch up on the odd little job. Anne and Margot understood. Father owned the company. He had to work hard for them to keep their beautiful home, to have nice things and of course to put food on the table and pay for clothes.

Anne's days were filled with school and fun. Everything was just fine. Until one morning in 1938 when she came to the breakfast table and she noticed Father had a stern expression on his face. With one hand he patted Mother's arm. She had obviously just been crying. Margot had gone very quiet.

'What's wrong?' Anne asked in fright.

'Don't worry. It's fine now,' Mother said.

'I want to know what happened!' Anne demanded. 'I can tell something has happened.'

Father answered quietly: 'Things are not going well in Germany. And that is hurting us, as we have always loved that country so much. That's all. Come now, eat something. It is almost time for school.'

'But Dad...'

'Enough, Anne.'

Mother tried to give Anne a little smile. Still, it did not

take away Anne's worry. She bet it had something to do with that man Hitler, the leader of Germany. But to her parents the subject was closed. They did not want to talk about it. Later Anne would discover what had really happened. Both her uncles had been arrested by the Nazis during a dreadful night of violence against Jewish people. A night which later became known as the *Kristallnacht*. Mother was worried sick.

A few weeks after that particular incident, Mother and Margot were getting ready to go to the synagogue. It was

Saturday morning. Father went to the office for a few more hours and Anne went to school, a usual thing back then. Mother and Father had invited a few Jewish acquaintances who lived in the area and also came from Germany to their home that afternoon, something they did quite regularly on Saturdays.

'Don't forget to get some *Kuchen* at the bakery, Otto!'

'Cake, Mum. Not *Kuchen*.'

'Of course, Anne,' Mother sighed. 'And I would like you to wash your hair when you come home from school and put on the *Kleid* I have put out for you.'

'Dress, you mean.'

'Anne, we're getting your point,' Father said sternly.

'How many people are you expecting this afternoon?' Anne asked.

'There will be some new people, Anne. And the regulars: Hannah's parents, Sanne's parents and my colleague Mr Van Pels with his wife. It's going to be nice and busy.'

'Will Miep and Jan be coming too?' Miep was Father's assistant at the office and she and her fiancé Jan had become friends of the family.

'I think so. I have invited them.'

'Great!' Anne said. She really liked Jan and Miep.

The morning at school flew by. Every Saturday they tidied, dusted and cleaned the classroom before going home. Some of the Jewish children, like Hannah, would not attend Saturday class as they went to the synagogue. But there were plenty of other children around. Some were Jewish like Anne, others Christian, or just not at all religious. Some children came from Germany, but that didn't matter at all. It was neither important nor talked about.

Anne's job was to open the door to their guests that afternoon. 'Don't forget to introduce yourself and shake hands,' Mother had said. Anne already knew most of the guests. Then a man and a woman she hadn't met before rang the doorbell.

'I'm Fritz Pfeffer,' the man said in a friendly voice. 'And this is my wife Charlotte Kaletta.' He spoke German.

'Welcome to our home,' Anne said politely. While she escorted the couple to greet her parents, she noticed that the atmosphere in the living room was not at all relaxed. There were indeed many people, as Father had predicted. But the faces of many guests were somber and the cake and nibbles were mostly left untouched.

Later Anne saw her mother putting her hand to her mouth while she was listening to Mr Pfeffer, obviously shocked by what he had just told her. Anne recalled her mother's words at the breakfast table some weeks earlier: 'Don't worry, my girl.' But to her it was obvious now that everyone was worried.

Still, Anne had plenty to be happy and cheerful about in the months that followed. Her birthday party, for example. June 1939 came around and it was only a few more days before Anne would turn ten. She was glad that her birthday was on a school day, because this meant she would see all her friends first and have a party later on at home. She would ask Hanneli and Sanne of course. Hanne, Sanne and Anne was what they were called. They had been good friends ever since they were toddlers. This was no surprise, as all three came from Jewish German families. She would also invite Ietje, Lucie, Martha and Mary. And Juultje and Kitty, of course. They were all good friends. Nine girls. It would be such fun!

One girl after another rang the doorbell that Monday afternoon, 12th June 1939. Anne welcomed them all at the door. 'That's how it should be done,' Mother had said. The weather was gorgeous. Anne was wearing her favourite dress with a floral print and a small white collar. Martha was wearing a festive bow in her hair and Mary topped that by having two. They were all in their summer dresses as the sun was beaming down on them. Anne was beaming too. She enjoyed being the centre of attention. Mother had baked a cake and had put drinks out. She softly started to sing: 'Happy birthday to you, happy birthday to you...' Anne's friends joined in and Anne was in her element. Then it was time for presents. Anne ripped off the paper. She adored presents! When all presents were unwrapped and the cake was eaten, it was time for games. Father asked all the girls to sit down in a circle.

'Why, Mr Frank?' Juultje asked cautiously.

'You'll see,' Anne's father answered mysteriously. 'And now, shoes off everyone!'

Some of the girls started to giggle. What could this mean?

Father picked up a large rug and put it over the girls' feet. 'And now,' he said, 'without seeing your feet, I will put on everyone's shoes again.'

'But that is impossible!' Ietje cried out.

'Just watch,' Father said and he picked up a shoe and started to rummage around under the rug feeling the different feet. It didn't take long for all the girls to fall over laughing. Anne looked at her father with admiration. What a wonderful man he was. Nobody had a father who was so much fun as her Pim, as she lovingly called him. Later that day Pim took a lovely photo of all the nine friends together. This surely was the best day ever. You'd wish every day would be like this.

Family

When Hitler and his Nazi Party came to power in January 1933, some members of Father's family had already left Germany. Aunt Leni and her family had moved to Switzerland a few years previously and Grandma Frank followed them in the autumn of 1933. Uncle Robert and his wife left for London in 1933, while Uncle Herbert had already moved to France in 1932. Mother's family, however, was still living in Germany. Anne's bachelor uncles, Julius and Walter Höllander, remained in the German city of Aachen near the Dutch border, as did Grandma Höllander.

From 1933 the Nazis ensured that life for Jewish people in Germany became ever more difficult. Jewish teachers lost their jobs. Jews were not allowed to marry non-Jews. In many German cities and villages there were signs put up saying Jews were not welcome. Many Jews tried to leave the country. They sought refuge in other countries, but that was not always easy. It was expensive and you had to find work and a new home.

Anne's parents tried everything to get Grandma Höllander to The Netherlands, but it was very difficult to get

From 1933 the Nazis ensured that life for Jewish people in Germany became ever more difficult.

the official documents. Then something terrible happened. In the night of 9 November 1938, Nazis all over Germany attacked Jews. They murdered more than a hundred Jews and arrested more than thirty thousand Jewish men. They vandalised Jewish shops, synagogues, houses and cemeteries. This night was called the Kristallnacht, or the Night of Broken Glass.

Anne's uncles Julius and Walter were also imprisoned a few days after that night. Uncle Julius was released fairly quickly because he had fought for Germany during World War 1. Uncle Walter, however, was sent to a concentration camp, a large prison with high fences and barbed wire. The family panicked. How could they organise Walter's release and after that, how could they get him and Uncle Julius out of Germany quickly? And Grandma? When would their application to get her to Amsterdam be granted?

Escape from the Nazis

'We've pulled it off, Edith!' It was the middle of November 1938. Father entered the living room, still wearing his winter coat. Mother looked at him nervously. She seemed to know immediately what he was talking about. Father nodded his head. 'I shall now try for Julius too. And Walter. Although it will be difficult.'

Mother looked anxious.

'Now, now, Edith. We mustn't give up hope,' Father whispered.

'What's the matter, Mum?' Anne asked, worried.

Mother didn't answer.

Father called for Margot who was in the bedroom. 'Please sit down for a moment,' he said. Anne and Margot both pulled up a chair and sat down at the table with their parents. 'We've had a message regarding Grandma. She was granted permission by the Dutch government to come and live with us.'

'Oh, that's just wonderful!' Anne exclaimed. 'When will she be arriving?'

'As soon as possible. Grandma first has to arrange a few things.'

Anne was happy, very happy. But Mother was quiet.

'Aren't you happy, Mum?' Anne asked.

Father answered instead. 'Mother would also like for Uncle Julius and Uncle Walter to leave Germany. But of course she is relieved that, for a start, Grandma can come and join us.'

Anne understood her mother better now. She knew that Grandma, Uncle Julius and Uncle Walter had had a difficult time in Germany. She often asked questions about it, but Father told her not to worry. It wasn't something a child had to know. She did know, however, that many of the problems were caused by this man Hitler, who now ruled Germany. He

hated Jews and many people agreed with his views. She also knew these so-called Nazis had arrested both her uncles and that only Uncle Julius had been set free. Uncle Walter was somewhere in Germany, in a concentration camp. Mother had eventually told the girls when they noticed she was becoming more and more worried about something.

'Go on,' Father said. 'You girls return to your room please, and then Mother and I will discuss the situation further. A lot of arrangements need to be made.'

Anne and Margot returned to the bedroom they shared and which was on the opposite side of the hallway to the living room. Margot closed the bedroom door, but Anne, always curious, put an ear to the door.

'Anne!' Margot said in exasperation. 'When the time is

right for Father and Mother to tell us more, they will!'

'You're such a goody two-shoes!' Anne grumbled. But she still moved away from the door.

That very day Father wrote a letter to an organisation helping Jewish refugees, requesting for Uncle Julius to be granted refuge in The Netherlands. In the letter he wrote that it was Uncle Julius' intention to travel to America and that he therefore would only be passing through. He, Otto Frank, would be willing to provide a roof over his head. All they could do for Uncle Walter was pray for a quick release. He would then follow Julius to America. At least, that was the plan.

Weeks went by. No news. But at the end of December 1938 they received good tidings.

'Walter has been released by the Nazis,' Father said with relief. Mother was so happy she burst into tears. 'He will soon come to The Netherlands,' Father continued.

'Is he coming to live here, Pim?' Anne asked. But Father said this would not be possible. In The Netherlands Uncle Walter would be going to a refugee camp.

'But why?' Margot asked. 'He is not allowed to stay in Holland,' Father explained. 'The Dutch government is of the opinion that it has already given enough asylum to German Jews. He will be staying there until he can go to another country.'

'So he is going to another kind of prison?' Anne concluded.

But Mother shook her head. 'It is only temporary, Anne. Both your uncles will travel to America.'

'America,' Anne said. 'Really? That's great!'

A few months later, in March 1939, Uncle Julius came to

Amsterdam. The organisation Father had written to had helped to make this possible. Uncle Julius was allowed to stay with his sister until his departure for America. Unfortunately, Uncle Walter did not yet get permission to enter America. The plan was changed. Uncle Julius would settle down in America first, and hope that Walter could follow later.

It was only a week later that Grandma Holländer also arrived in Amsterdam. 'Grandma!' Anne cheered when she heard the key in the lock of the front door. Mother and Margot came to the hallway. There was Father with Grandma. Anne jumped up and down excitedly. Grandma ascended the steep stairs slowly. She looked up and smiled at Anne, who was a bit taken aback. Grandma looked so old! Much older than she remembered.

She hugged Grandma tightly. 'It is so nice to see you, Grandma!' Mother also gave Grandma a hug and a kiss and helped her taking off her coat. Uncle Julius seemed relieved his mother had arrived without any problems.

Margot helped Father carry the two suitcases to the part of the living room that was now transformed into Grandma's room. 'Look Grandma. Here's your bed.' Anne gestured. Grandma nodded gratefully, but Anne noticed sadness in her eyes.

'Just give Grandma some space now, girls,' Mother said. Anne and Margot understood what Mother was trying to say and left for their room.

'I don't understand. I thought it was nice for Grandma to stay with us?' Anne mused.

'She had to leave everything behind, Anne,' Margot answered softly.

Everything? Anne thought. Everything? Uncle Julius and
Grandma had only been carrying a few suitcases each. Did
they have to leave the furniture, the books, the paintings and
all their other belongings behind? Or would they arrive
later? That evening Anne couldn't help but fire question

after question at her father, who responded calmly. 'Listen, Anne. Uncle Julius is leaving for America. So will Uncle Walter, we hope. Grandma is staying with us. That is the most important thing. They are all safe.'

'But, Pim...'

'Trust me Anne, those things are not important.'

'But...'

Father shook his head. End of conversation.

The next morning Uncle Julius got ready to leave. He would first take the train to Rotterdam, where he would board a large vessel called *Veendam*. Then the doorbell rang. Mother opened the front door and came back with a big smile on her face. 'Julius, look who has come to say goodbye.'

'Uncle Walter!' Anne let out.

Everyone was delighted to see Walter. Father had been able to arrange a few hours leave from the refugee camp to enable Walter to say farewell to his brother. And to embrace his mother, who he hadn't seen in months. And of course to see his sister, Otto and the girls. Uncle Walter smiled. He was very happy to see everyone again. No, of course life in a refugee camp wasn't great, he said. 'But now Mother is here in Amsterdam. Julius is crossing the pond and I will surely follow him soon. We have all escaped the Nazis!'

Time came to say goodbye to Julius. 'I will write to you all as often as I can,' he said while he took his mother in a bear hug. 'Look after Mother,' he told his sister quietly, who nodded but seemed too sad to answer. 'Girls,' he addressed Anne and Margot as cheerfully as he could muster: 'Keep growing big, smart and beautiful! One day I hope to see you in America.'

'Yes!' Anne said happily. 'That would be wonderful, Uncle Julius.'

Julius hugged his brother tightly. 'Hang on in there,' he said. 'I hope you can follow soon.' Uncle Walter nodded. Uncle Julius softly squeezed Grandma's hand one more time, picked up his bags and walked down the stairs with Father. Anne ran to the window to see them off. Margot and Uncle Walter followed her. But Mother and Grandma sat down in a chair, neither of them saying a word.

One day that spring Anne returned from school. She rushed over to Grandma to tell her about the fun things she had done that day. Skipping rope, the joke they played on Miss Godron, the difficult sums she'd solved. And the stories Hanneli had told, and Mary and Juultje and Ietje. Grandma enjoyed her stories and always listened patiently. But that day she interrupted Anne after a few minutes.

'There is a surprise for you, Anne. A letter.'

'A letter? Where?'

'I've put it on your writing desk.'

'I'm going to have a look straight away,' she said while already walking towards the bedroom.

On the writing desk at the window she found two letters, one addressed to Margot and one for her. 'Miss Anne Frank', it said. 'Miss'. Funny! '37 Merwede Square, Amsterdam'. Posted in Amsterdam, Anne noted from the postmark on the stamp. But the best thing of all was the tiny little word written in the top left corner: Personal. That made it a very special letter indeed.

Anne knew the handwriting. It was a letter from Pim. She

opened the envelop by tearing it with her finger. The letter began with the date: 12 May 1939. Tomorrow's date. Tomorrow was her parent's wedding anniversary and her father's fiftieth birthday. On this special day, he had obviously decided to also give her something special. This wasn't something uncommon in their family: they often wrote each other a letter or a poem on an anniversary or birthday. No doubt, Mother would get a letter too. '*My sweet little Anne.*' Her eyes raced over Father's lines. She laughed, she giggled, it brought a lump in her throat. What a sweet letter! She read every sentence again.

'*You do not always make life easy for us, Anne,*' the letter said. '*It would be good if you would use the word "but" just that little bit less.*' Anne had to smile. When Father, Mother, Grandma or the teacher said something, she indeed often countered that with a 'but' after they were finished. She always needed to know more. Or she wanted to correct them. She had to learn to pause and count to ten, to think before speaking, Father noted. There were plenty of people who were quite allergic to her 'buts'. And also, adults often had good reasons not to go into detail. There really was no need for her to know everything.

Anne continued reading. '*Don't worry though, as long as you remain a good and kind person at heart.*' Such tender words. Very sweet! Then she read the last sentence. '*That you may always continue to smile, the smile that brightens your life, ours and that of others.*' Father had signed the letter with 'Yours, Pim'.

Anne pressed the letter against her chest. This was the most beautiful letter she had ever received. She would keep it forever, she decided. Forever.

The summer holidays of 1939 started. After the holidays Anne would go to year six, the last grade before secondary education. They couldn't afford to travel, but there were enough fun things to do that summer. They went to the beach, friends came over to play regularly and there were plenty of parties. The girls were also busy writing in each other's poetry albums. These were pretty little books in which friends wrote a poem or verse in order for them to remember each other in later life. Juultje, one of Anne's classmates, had been given one of these by Kitty, another girl

from school, for her birthday. It was now Anne's turn to write something for Juultje and the album was lying on her writing desk.

'Mum, do you have a photograph of me I can use?'

'What do you want to use it for?'

'For Juultje's poetry album.'

Mother took a large sheet with small passport photographs from the cupboard and looked for a pair of scissors.

'No, not those! Those are last year's! I want a recent one.'

'These are fine, Anne. The more recent ones we are sending to the family.'

'But I look like a toddler in that picture.'

'It was taken last year, Anne. You can have this one or none at all!'

Anne took the photograph and went grumpily to her writing desk. She opened the album. Kitty, Hanneli and Ietje had already written something and all three had added a small photograph with their poem. Looking at these, she figured her photo wasn't that bad. It had to do. She picked up her fountain pen and tapped on her desk. What would she write? Tap-tap. Pom-pom.

Then she knew. As neatly as she could she wrote:

'Sweet Juultje
What shall I write on this sheet of paper though?
But wait, sweet Juultje, I know
Wishing you health and in life all the best
Be generous and brave and very blessed
And always think what destiny will bring
Because every cloud has a silver lining

To remember your friend
Anne Frank.'

Done. And a good job too, she thought to herself. She waited
for the ink to dry and wrote into the corners of the left page,
the one she had stuck her photo on in the centre:
'For – Get – Me – Not.'

War

36   Even though the Frank family enjoyed being in The Netherlands, Anne's parents worried greatly about the future and the things that would lie ahead. They had heard terrible stories of Jews being attacked, taken prisoner and murdered. A man who allowed something like that to happen would surely be capable of much worse. Perhaps he would even go to war.

This premonition proved to be true when the German army invaded its neighbouring country Poland on 1 September 1939. England and France responded angrily and declared war on Germany. Hitler, however, did not seem to be impressed by this, as in April 1940 his army also attacked Denmark and Norway. This was reason enough for Anne's parents to become really worried. The Netherlands had always been of the opinion to stay neutral in this conflict, meaning that it would not intervene with the different parties at war, as it had done in World War 1. But now The

Perhaps Hitler would even go to war.

Netherlands were surrounded by countries that were
already at war with Germany. Would it be able to maintain
this position? After all, the Dutch army had been preparing
itself for war for months should the German army attack.

Anne's parents and grandmother agreed not to tell Anne
and Margot of their worries. They had to try to keep their
spirits up, no matter what might happen!

Airport bombings

'Look, Anne.' Father and Anne sat at the table. In front of them was an atlas. 'This is where Uncle Julius and Uncle Walter now live, in the American state of Massachusetts.' Father pointed to the east coast of the United States. Uncle Walter had left for America some months previously. They'd managed to compile the necessary paperwork and everyone had been very relieved. 'This here is New York,' Father continued. 'I worked there for a short while before I met your mother.' Anne nodded. Father had told her these stories before. His finger traced the map to the centre. 'And this is the state of Iowa. That's where your pen pal lives.'

'How far is it from Iowa to Massachusetts?' Anne asked.

'Oh, I would estimate approximately two thousand kilometres.'

'Wow! What a distance!'

'What is the name of the city again where your pen pal lives?'

Anne took Juanita Wagner's letter from the envelope. Her eyes scanned the English sentences she had just been reading with Father. Yes, there it was. Danville, near Burlington, Iowa. Anne and Father studied the map again.

'There!' Anne had spotted it. Well, Burlington at least.
Danville was probably too small to be mentioned on a map.
The farm where Juanita and her older sister Betty Ann lived
with their family was somewhere near there.

'I just love it that Margot's pen pal Betty Ann has a younger
sister, Pim. Now she can write to Betty Ann and I can write to
Juanita.'

Father agreed. 'It is wonderful, Anne.'

'Do you have time to help me out later? I would not know
how else to write a letter in English.'

'Just draft it first.'

Anne went to the writing desk in her bedroom to start
drafting the letter straight away. 'Monday, 29 April 1940', she
wrote. She wrote about Father, Mother, Margot and
Grandma. About school and about her collection of picture

postcards. And about her friend Mary Bos who had moved to New York. It turned out to be a nice, long and inviting letter. She decided to add a picture postcard of Amsterdam and a photo of herself.

After Father had translated her letter into English, Anne neatly transcribed it onto pretty light blue writing paper. Would Juanita write back soon? She hoped she would! Anne thought it was wonderful to have a pen pal. Perhaps Juanita would also include a photo of herself? She sure was curious about what Juanita looked like.

'Do you think there will be a letter from Juanita soon?' Anne asked after a week. It was a beautiful spring evening in May. It was bedtime and Father was entering her bedroom for her goodnight kiss.

'I don't think so, my girl. Things don't move that fast. I guess it will take another week or two.'

'Hmmmm,' Anne mumbled.

'Sweet dreams.'

Father closed the door and it wasn't long before Anne fell into a deep sleep.

That night she was woken by a strange, heavy noise. She sat up. Margot opened her eyes too. Just then there was thud, somewhere outside. It wasn't close, but that didn't make it less scary. Another one. And again, followed by a heavy droning sound that seemed very close.

'That isn't thunder, is it?' Anne asked, trembling. She didn't like thundery weather. Lightning in particular was very scary. However, there was no lightning now. This was different. Before Margot could answer her question, a very loud roaring sounded just above their heads. Anne jumped

out of bed and ran to her parents' bedroom. Father was already out of bed and Mother had a fearful expression on her face.

'What is it, Pim?' Anne asked, her voice trembling as she held onto him tightly.

'I don't know, my little one,' he tried to reassure her. But Anne noticed the worry in his voice.

They heard some stumbling in the hallway and saw Grandma standing in the doorway. She had woken up too. Father broke away from Anne and walked to the window. He opened the curtains. It was a clear night. There was not much to see. Then, again, a terrifying and thundering noise approached. Anne, Margot, Mother and Grandma all walked over to the window. Then they knew. These were planes. Many planes.

'What are they doing here, Pim?' Anne asked in a voice full of fear.

Father didn't say anything. Nothing at all.

'*Du meine Güte*,' Mother sighed, meaning something like 'Oh my God!'

Anne started to cry. 'Please say something!'

Father went over to Anne and hugged her tight. 'We don't know, Anne. Let's try to stay calm.'

It was almost four in the morning on Friday May 10, 1940 and everywhere in Amsterdam, fearful people were looking out of their windows. Anne and her family watched the planes, dozens perhaps. It was impossible to count them. They heard one thud after another. If they focused their eyes, they could see smoke rising above the roofs.

'Schiphol airport,' was all Father said.

'Does this mean war, Dad?' Margot asked quietly.

'I don't know, girl,' he answered. 'But this doesn't sound good.'

Anne's gaze went from Father to Margot and back again. War? But what did that mean?

Father walked to the living room and turned on the radio. Perhaps some news would be broadcast on the events outside. But there was no news.

For two hours the planes continued to fly over. Around six in the morning all went quiet. But who could sleep now? Mother made breakfast, but nobody could eat.

At eight in the morning, news finally arrived. All five went dead quiet when the newsreader announced he would read a message from Her Majesty the Queen. 'My countrymen,' he started. Then a story followed that did not make much sense to Anne. 'A sudden attack on our country,' she heard, 'despite the solemn declaration that the neutral position of our country would be respected.' What did that mean? 'The government and I will continue to do our duty.' Then the message was over. Mother had tears in her eyes and had put a hand on Grandma's arm. Father was pensively staring ahead. Margot too was awfully quiet.

'I don't understand,' Anne broke the silence. 'So what exactly did he say?'

Father sighed. 'He said,' he started. Then he had to cough. 'He said that the German army has attacked The Netherlands.'

'So what will happen next, Dad?'

'I don't know,' he whispered. 'We shall have to wait and see.'

'But,' Anne started. Father shook his head. He looked sad.

That morning Father walked Anne to school, but on arrival they heard that the schools would stay closed until further notice. On their way home they saw many people talking to one another in the street. But apart from that, it seemed a normal day. No planes, no thunderous thuds in the distance.

Later that morning Anne wanted to see Hanneli. Or Sanne. But Mother told her to stay in the house.

'Why? The weather is beautiful and right now, nothing is happening out there!'

'No buts, Anne. Just do as I say.'

'Can I call them?'

'The phone line is dead.'

'Why?'

'I don't know, Anne.'

'Come on,' Grandma said as cheerfully as possible. 'Let's play a game.'

It was a very strange day. Mother was tense and nervous. Despite everything, Father went to the office. Margot did her homework and Anne and Grandma entertained themselves with games. Outside the sun was shining. But when Father returned home later that day, he looked very worried.

When twilight came that evening, lights were switched on only after Father and Mother had shut all the curtains tightly.

Father had heard on the radio that everyone was asked to keep their homes as dark as possible. To ensure that not a ray of light would be seen from the outside, they stuck strips of paper to the windowpanes. This way German pilots would not be able to see where people lived and would not be able to identify important sites in the city to bomb. Father didn't explain all this though. He only said it would help the Dutch soldiers. 'The Dutch troops are fighting the German attackers bravely,' he calmly explained. 'The battle isn't over yet.'

Even so, they were afraid when the air-raid alarm went off in the city for a very long time the next day. And the day after that. And the following day as well. Planes continued to fly over the city and every now and then loud bangs could be heard in the distance. What was happening? Why didn't this stop? The Dutch soldiers would get rid of their attackers, wouldn't they?

On 15 May, five nights after that first frightening night of air raids, Father called for Anne and Margot. 'The Dutch army has surrendered,' he said while taking their hands. 'Our Queen and her family as well as the government have fled to England. From now on the Germans will be in charge.'

Anne didn't know what to think of this. 'Is that a bad thing?'

'We have to stay calm, Anne. That is the only thing we can do. Okay?'

Anne nodded. She was ever so slightly confused. Would she be able to play outside again? Or not? And would school re-open and would she be able to go and see her friends?

Two weeks passed. The German troops had entered the city with tanks. The streets of Amsterdam were patrolled

regularly by large army trucks filled with German soldiers. In the shops they also occasionally ran into German soldiers carrying large guns. It looked scary. Sometimes they marched with their heavy noisy boots through the streets. But the schools had opened again.

'I don't really notice the fact that the Germans are in charge now, do you?' Anne asked Hannah one afternoon. They were comparing their movie star picture collections in Anne's room.

Hannah went quiet for a minute. Then she said: 'Can you keep a secret?'

Anne nodded with a stern face.

'I'm not supposed to tell,' her friend wavered.

'I swear,' Anne said solemnly.

Hannah sat really close to Anne and whispered very softly:

'My parents shredded lots of papers and threw them in the toilet.'

'But why, Hanneli?'

'Father didn't say, but I think they contained information that could turn out to be dangerous.' Anne frowned. 'Things Hitler would not approve of,' Hannah clarified. 'Things that could spell trouble if the Nazis found them.'

'Were you there?'

Hannah nodded. 'I repeatedly had to flush the toilet.'

Anne's eyes widened. Now she whispered too: 'Sanne said her father had burned some books, because the Nazis would not approve of them.'

'Are you scared?' Hannah asked.

'Fairly. But Father and Mother tell us there is no need to be afraid. They think it won't take long.'

'That's what my parents say as well,' said Hannah. 'Still, they act awfully nervous.'

Anne nodded. Her mother was nervous too. But Father remained calm and went to the office every day as if nothing had happened.

That summer Anne was still hoping to receive a letter from Juanita in America. It never came. 'It probably has something to do with the war,' Father said whenever she asked. Anne thought it weird. Germany and America weren't enemies, were they? Now with this war, many things had changed. But thankfully also many things had remained the same. On days when it was sunny the Frank family would head for the beach, as they did every summer. On other days Anne would go to see her friends, or they also liked to come and play at her house. After the summer holidays Anne went to the last class in primary school. There were days she almost forgot there was a war going on. But at night, when she heard the German planes flying over the city heading for England, she would quietly cry tears of fear. Then Father would comfort her by softly stroking her hair. 'It will be alright, Anne. Don't you worry. We are here.' Sometimes, when she would enter the living room unexpectedly, a silence would fall and Father and Mother would stop their conversation. When she asked if anything was the matter, they would assure her that all was well.

Six months after the start of the occupation Father moved his company, which was prospering despite the war, to a new building. The building was near the Wester tower, a historic landmark of Amsterdam, at 263 Prinsengracht. It was an old, narrow, long canal building. When Anne first visited this building, it felt like an exciting maze. Lots of stairs and lots of hallways! And just when you thought you'd seen it all, there was another whole building, like a house, at the back of the office. A perfect place to play hide-and-seek!

1941 came around. Just after New Year, Anne returned home from school quite upset. 'Children on the playground say that Jewish people are not allowed to go to the cinema anymore, Mum. It's not true, is it?'

Mother kissed Anne and calmly replied, 'Father and I heard the same thing, Anne. But surely there are worse things that can happen.'

'How can you say that! You know how much I like to go to the movies!'

'You can invite your friends for our movie afternoons as often as you like. Father will play them at home, okay?'

'But that isn't the same!'

'We'll have to make do, Anne!' But Anne clenched her fists.

What a silly thing. Not being allowed to go to the cinema just because she was Jewish.

On a sunny Sunday afternoon in spring of 1941 Father had to do some odd jobs at the office. 'Can I tag along, Pim? Please, please?' Anne asked in a sweet voice.

'What do you want to do there?'

'Oh nothing special, just walk around, playing a bit.'

Father looked at her, smiling. Anne knew she had won him over.

'Okay, why not?' Father said. 'But ask a friend to come along, because I really need to do some work and cannot be with you all the time. Then you have at least someone to play with.'

Anne invited Hannah. The three of them took the tram later that day and soon arrived at the Prinsengracht offices where Opekta and Pectacon, Father's companies, were situated. Anne didn't know that, at that time, Father was no longer officially owner of the company. The Nazis did not allow Jewish people to have their own businesses. That was why he had appointed Mr Kleiman, one of his most trusted employees, as director on paper. Jan Gies, Miep's fiancé, and Victor Kugler took over Pectacon and changed the name to Gies & Co. Father went to the office less often, but still took all the important decisions.

Anne knew exactly what kind of companies Father had. They produced a powder and fluid that you could add to fresh fruit to produce your own jam or jelly. Herbs and spices were mixed to enhance the taste of meat. You could smell all kinds of things on entering the building, particularly downstairs in the warehouse.

'No silly tricks, young ladies,' said Father as he opened the door to his own office.

'But we can look around, can't we, Pim?' Anne asked. 'Perhaps play with the phones a bit?'

Father laughed. 'Look,' he said pointing at a small protruding rod on the telephone that sat on Miep's desk. 'If you push this rod, you can call the other phones in this office. Miep's number is one. Mr Kugler's is four.' He pointed at the round disk with numbers on the phone. 'If you push the rod down first and then dial the number, the phone in the other office will ring. Do you get it?'

The girls beamed. That would be fun, to phone each other! 'I'm going to Mr Kugler's room,' Anne said. 'You can call me there, Hanneli!'

Anne ran to Mr Kugler's room and sat behind his heavy wooden desk. She picked up a pencil and stared earnestly at a piece of paper as if waiting for a very important phone call.

Tring, tring, tring!

Anne picked up the receiver and held it to her ear. 'A very good afternoon, this is...'

'Hihihi.' On the other end of the line, Hannah was laughing out loud.

'What's so funny?' Anne asked indignantly.

'A very good afternoon, haha. Nobody says that! A very good afternoon. Haha!'

'Well, I'm just pretending to be Mr Kugler. So, I'm important in the company.'

'But do you really think he would say it that way?'

Anne pictured Father's quiet and modest colleague. Perhaps Hanneli had a point. He probably would act

differently. 'Alright then,' she said in the receiver. 'I'll hang up and you can call me again.'

Anne tapped impatiently on the desk until the phone rang again.

'Opekta, this is Mr Kugler, good afternoon.'

Silence.

'Is anyone there?'

Giggling, coughing and then Hannah's voice, but very posh. 'This is Mrs Van Castricum speaking.'

'What can I do for you, Mrs Van Castricum?'

'I would like to file a complaint, haha.'

'Is that so, Mrs Van Castricum, and what would this complaint be, if I may ask?'

'Well,' Hanneli laughed, 'I was making strawberry jam this afternoon,' she continued to giggle, 'but it has gone terribly wrong. There was so much splashing there's now even some on the ceiling.'

'Okay, that's it, Hanneli. Just play serious pretend here.'

And so they continued to have some afternoon fun.

A whole year had passed since the German invasion. The summer holiday of 1941 was approaching and Anne, as well as Hannah, were told that they would both stay at primary school for another year. Miss Kuperus thought this wise judging by their grades, particularly if they wanted to go to grammar school. First they would enjoy a lovely holiday though. Chatting, reading, playing. All the things they loved doing, except... swimming in the pool. Just before summer the Nazis had announced a new decree: Jewish people were no longer allowed to use the public swimming pools. Father and Mother pretended not to care much. So swimming was not an option. It couldn't be helped. Fortunately, there were plenty of other nice things to do. But at night in bed, more and more often, Anne would wonder what the next new decree would be.

Regulations

Summer of 1941 arrived. The Nazis slowly continued to make life harder for Jews. More and more things were gradually taken away from them. More anti-Jewish regulations were introduced, changing the lives of children as well. There already was an order that forbade Jewish people from going to the market, the cinema or public swimming pools. An important new regulation, however, stipulated that Jewish children were only allowed to attend Jewish schools. This meant that Anne and Margot both had to change schools. As a result they were no longer seeing their non-Jewish friends regularly. This made them very sad.

Even very common everyday activities, such as driving a car, taking the train, bus or tram or buying things in non-Jewish shops were forbidden. Libraries were off-limits for Jews too. Participating in sports like ice-skating was also prohibited. Many Jews lost their jobs.

Anne's father wrote letter after letter to ask permission for the family to leave for the United States. Cuba even. He was desperate, even though he did not let on. But all his efforts were in vain. They could not leave The Netherlands.

An important new regulation stipulated that Jewish children were only allowed to attend Jewish schools.

In May 1942 Jewish people were made to wear the Star of David and were no longer allowed to visit non-Jews. They became increasingly isolated. Just as the German occupier had intended.

No Jews allowed

'Are you ready, Anne?' Margot called out to Anne, who was still in their bedroom.

'In a minute.'

Anne's bed was covered in clothes. She had chosen what to wear. But which coat would go with her outfit? This one? Or the other one? She'd wear those shoes. No, no, change of plan: the other ones after all. They matched the coat better. That is to say…. They didn't match the dress she was wearing. Decisions, decisions. She didn't know what to wear.

'Come on. I've been waiting for you for ages.'

'Alright, alright!'

Anne made up her mind and walked into the hallway. Margot grabbed her coat from the coat rack. Mother came out of the kitchen and handed them a lunch bag each. 'Be careful, Anne,' she said. 'Stay with Margot.'

'I'm not a baby,' Anne replied grumpily. This summer had seen her twelfth birthday and she thought she was old enough not to do anything silly.

It was the first day of the school year 1941–1942 and everything turned out not quite as she had thought before the holidays had started. Then Anne was told that she would have to stay another year at primary school as her grades had not been up to scratch. But now she was going to secondary school after all. A Jewish secondary school. This was because Father and Mother had received a letter that summer notifying them that all Jewish children had to go to special Jewish schools. This meant she could not return to her old school. The same for Margot. Before the summer holidays she had attended a local authority grammar school for girls. Now they would both go to the brand new Jewish grammar school, a ten-minute bike ride from home.

'Are we going now?' Margot asked impatiently. Anne nodded her head.

'See you later, girls,' Mother said. But Anne was already down the stairs. It was bleak and dark outside. Not unusual for an October day. Getting every Jewish child into a special Jewish school had taken more time than anticipated, resulting in a particularly long summer holiday.

Margot cycled fast. 'Slow down!' Anne shouted out of breath.

'We don't want to get wet, do we?' Margot responded. And as she said it, the first drops of rain started to fall. Before long rain was pouring down. 'Faster!' Margot shouted. 'Otherwise we'll be late.'

They soon arrived at the Jewish grammar school. It was a large imposing building. Anne had been there a week earlier to get her book list and to hear which class she would be attending. She had been very relieved when she found out she would be in the same class as Hanneli. Now, however, the large announcement board at the entrance revealed she had been transferred to another group.

'Now I'm not with Hanneli anymore,' she said dispirited to Margot. 'I don't know anybody.'

'I'm sure it is going to be alright,' Margot reassured her while she started walking down the corridor. 'I have to go. Good luck!'

Feeling a little uneasy, Anne walked towards the room where class 1L2 was to gather. She sat down at the assigned table. During the third hour however Anne's bold streak returned and she approached the PA teacher who seemed

friendly enough. 'Miss,' she said politely. 'My best friend Hannah Goslar attends class 1L1 and I would really love to be in the same class as her. Here I hardly know anybody.'

The teacher smiled at Anne. 'I'll see what I can do.'

The next hour Anne found herself in Geography. She looked up from her book when the door opened. There was Hanneli! Anne beamed when her friend sat down next to her. Sorted!

'See you tomorrow!' she shouted at the end of that first school day after Hanneli, who was walking home with Ilse, another friend. Anne walked to the bike shed, picked up her bike and started her journey home. Not far ahead she spotted a girl she recognised. It was Jacqueline, one of the girls from her new class. She also turned the corner, into the same road Anne had to ride. Anne decided to pick up some speed. 'Jacqueline!' The girl looked over her shoulder. 'Wait for me!' Anne now cycled as fast as she could. 'Where are you going?' she shouted.

'Straight ahead.'

'Excellent. That means we can cycle to school together from now on.' Anne noticed Jacqueline was looking at her in surprise. 'I'm in your class,' she said. 'Did you not notice me?' Jacqueline shook her head. 'I'm Anne,' she said. 'Anne Frank.' Jacqueline gave her a friendly smile. Anne decided there and then that this would be her new friend. No doubt about it.

'Where do you live?'

'In the Hunze street,' Jacqueline said.

'I know it,' Anne said enthusiastically. After all, Miep and Jan also lived in the Hunze street. 'I live close by, at Merwede Square. Would you like to come over to my house?'

'I think my mother might get worried.'

'Oh, could you not give her a call?'

Jacqueline nodded her head. 'Okay.'

They went up the stairs together where Mother was waiting for them. 'This is my new friend from school, Mum,' Anne said. 'Her name is Jacquie.'

Mother shook hands with Jacqueline. 'How was your first day at school?'

'Oh, fine!' Anne said cheerfully. 'I'll tell you something

funny about Hanneli later. Ah, here comes Moortje!' Anne picked up the black cat. 'Isn't she sweet? Come on, we'll get her some food!'

She then introduced Jacqueline to Grandma, who was sitting on a chair by the window. Anne kissed her. She looked so fragile ever since her operation that summer. But she was still as sweet as ever. Later that afternoon Jacqueline also met Anne's father and Margot. Anne really enjoyed Jacqueline's company. She even invited her to stay for dinner that same afternoon. 'And tomorrow we'll go to your place,' she decided on their goodbye.

From that day onwards Jacqueline and Anne were inseparable. Jacqueline also liked Hannah, and Anne and Jacqueline in turn also got along fine with Hannah's friend Ilse. Sanne, with whom Anne had spent her summer holiday, went to a different school. But that didn't stop her from joining this new club of friends.

Now that the German occupier was isolating Jewish children from others by sending them to special schools, feelings of unrest started to creep in. After all, they did not feel different from other children. At school, not only the children, but the teachers too, were Jewish. They had all lost their jobs with their old schools, dismissed for being Jewish. For everyone, the Jewish grammar school was a new school. Nevertheless, Anne thought the Jewish school was great. It was a school where she had fun, got homework and.... got punished.

'Anne Frank!' Mr Keesing looked angrily at Anne. 'In the last hour I have asked you several times to stop chatting.' Anne looked at her maths teacher a little guiltily. Judging from his face, she had gone too far. 'I have warned you more than enough now. I want you to write me an essay with the title "A chatterbox". Two pages. On my desk tomorrow.'

'Yes, sir. I apologise, sir.'

That afternoon Anne was pensively sitting at her writing desk. What on earth could she write about 'A chatterbox' that would fill two whole pages? Hmmm. She stared ahead. And then it dawned on her. She would proof she was the victim of an inherited characteristic. All women chat. It is in their genes. They can't help it. Her mother talked a lot, so she must have inherited this from her.

Anne quietly smiled when she handed in her essay. But

her happy mood ceased the following day, when, after again being warned for chatting, a second essay was asked for punishment. This time the title would have to be: 'A chatter-box forever'. When this second assignment also failed to subdue Anne, a third one followed. The class sniggered when Mr Keesing gave her the title of her third essay: 'Quack, Quack, Quack, Miss Cackle said'. And Anne? Together with Sanne she composed a pretty poem about a mother duck, a father swan and three ducklings quacking away. Mr Keesing tried to keep a straight face when he read the poem, but his eyes twinkled. How could you stay angry with a pupil that showed so much spirit and humour!

Winter came around and Anne looked forward to going ice-skating with her friends. She really enjoyed that and had done it as often as she had been able to in winters gone by. She had dreams that one day she would be able to skate just as well as her cousin Bernd who lived in Basel. She looked forward to going ice-skating with him once this war was over. They would surprise everyone with the tricks they could do on their skates! But Father had to disappoint her.

'Remember that regulation, Anne... the one they announced back in September...' he started.

'You mean the one in which it is prohibited for people like us to go to the parks. Or to the zoos. Or to the theatres. Or the libraries.'

Father nodded his head. 'That also includes the ice rink, Anne. I'm afraid you can't go skating. I'm sorry.'

'But, why...'

'I don't have the answers, Anne.' He grabbed both her hands. 'Let's hope that this time next year, the war will be over. Then you will be back on your skates again.'

That evening Anne could not eat. She had lost her appetite. She missed the swimming pool, the cinema, the library. Not being allowed to ice-skate however... It felt horrible. Just like those terrible signs she encountered in the city, saying: 'Prohibited for Jews'. She felt angry and scared. Just as she was fearful at night when she heard the planes flying over their house. This dreadful war.

But more sad things happened in the months that

followed. Grandma Höllander's health deteriorated. She passed away at the end of January 1942. Anne was very sad. She knew, of course, that Grandma had not been well, you could tell just by looking at her, but that she might actually die was not something that had crossed her mind. How could it: Grandma was such a big part of their lives!

To forget their worries and sadness Anne and Margot's parents organised fun things to do, as much as they were able to.

'Jacquie, I can invite children from school to come over and watch a movie,' Anne beamed one afternoon. 'That will be such fun! Father will borrow a projector from the office and is going to rent a movie.'

Jacqueline was very enthusiastic. 'You know what would be fun too?'

Anne looked questioningly at her friend.

'Let's make cinema tickets for everyone. Including seating numbers and all.'

'Yes!' Anne smiled. 'And we'll write on them: No admittance without this ticket.'

'Let's,' Jacqueline giggled. They set to work straight away.

One anti-Jewish regulation after another was announced during that time. At the end of April 1942, it was announced that all Jews older than six years of age had to wear a Star of David.

'There's four for each of us,' Mother said, showing Anne and Margot the yellow stars made of fabric. They were as big as the palm of a hand and had 'Jew' in large letters stamped on it. The law said that the star had to be visible at all times and therefore had to be sewn chest high on the left side of their clothes. Now everyone would know you were Jewish. Jews over the age of fourteen already had a large, fat 'J' stamped in their passports, which they were obliged to carry at all times. But at least, these could be put in your pocket or in your bag. But that star: it was obvious for everyone to see. Good people recognised you immediately, but worse, also people with a dislike for Jews. Not only Dutch Nazis, but sometimes 'normal' Dutch people too. They were called NSBers, after the political party they belonged to. These people were happy with the German occupation. They believed in the things Hitler tried to achieve, in his methods and his followers. Parents of some of the children that had been in Anne's class previously were members of the NSB. That was hard to comprehend.

Summer came. For two years it had been a time of war in The Netherlands and Anne was almost thirteen.

'Do you know what you would like for a birthday present?' Father asked.

'Well...' she said. 'I've seen something in the window of Blankevoort.'

Father smiled. A book. Of course. Anne loved reading.

'It is a diary,' Anne said. 'A red-white chequered one with a tiny lock. Very pretty. That's the one I would like.'

'That is a beautiful present,' Mother said. 'Let's buy it together.'

'It suits you,' Margot added. Anne was happy. She would get the present she really, really wanted.

Friday June 12th arrived. Her last birthday had been a little disappointing due to Grandma's illness. The year before that

the war had just started. This time though, Anne was ready for a party!

And what a party it would turn out to be! Anne was delighted with all the presents she received that Friday, but the diary: that was something very special. She could hardly wait to write her first entry. But first, a normal school day awaited her, when she could treat the class to homemade cookies. After school, Jacqueline, Hannah, Sanne and Ilse stopped by to have cake. And more people came around. Peter van Pels, for example, the son of friends of her parents. He brought some milk chocolate. And Hello Silberberg, a boy with whom she had become friends over the past few weeks, rang the doorbell with six carnations.

'No, I'm not in love,' Anne told her friends after he had left.

'Of course you're not,' Sanne giggled.

'No way!' Ilse added to this.

'Why would we think such a thing?' Jacquie said with a big grin on her face.

'The very idea!' Hanneli continued. They all laughed out loud.

That Sunday many girls and boys from Anne's class came to Merwede Square to watch the thrilling movie about the dog Rin-Tin-Tin. Jacqueline, Hanneli and Ilse bought Anne a lovely book and a few other girls gave books too. Nanny presented Anne with a pretty bookmark. Very useful indeed!

They had a lovely Sunday afternoon. They enjoyed being

together, eating Mother's strawberry pie and playing Father's games. The fact that a new regulation had decreed that they were not allowed to buy vegetables from non-Jews – and this just on Anne's birthday – was something none of them wanted to think about that day. Nor did they discuss the Star of David they were all now wearing and which had to be properly stitched onto their clothing. Today, for one tiny moment, the war didn't exist. The curtains were closed. Outside there was war. Inside, it was time for Rin-Tin-Tin!

Fear

68   Two weeks after Anne's fun-filled thirteenth birthday party,
rumours were circulating that all Jews would be sent to
work camps in Germany. Today we know that almost all Jews
that went to these so-called work camps were eventually
murdered. But back then people didn't know. They might
have heard stories, but couldn't believe they could possibly
be true. Some Jews thought it best to obey orders from the
Nazis in order to have a chance of surviving the war. When
called up for a work camp, they went. But there were also
Jews who were suspicious and afraid they would never
return from these work camps. All the rules and regulations
already enforced by the Nazis did not have their best
interests at heart and they were not to be trusted. After all,
why were the elderly, children, the sick and handicapped
people also called up? How would they be able to work?
What would their jobs be? Anne's father was one of those

Anne's father was one of those who
had decided they would not be sent to
a work camp.

who had decided they would not be sent to a work camp.
For months he had been secretly preparing a hiding place for
his family.

The secret hiding place

It was as normal a Sunday as any, that 5th of July 1942. The weather was lovely and in the morning Anne took her time to write in her diary. Hello also popped in. After lunch she nestled in the deckchair on the flat roof at the back of the house, enjoying the sunshine. She was in a good mood. She had had her school report a few days earlier and it had been better than she had expected. And now the summer holiday had started. Wonderful! Hello would return after dinner, he had said. Well, let's wait and see.

'Anne!'

Anne looked up from her book and saw Margot standing in the open window looking as pale as a sheet. 'Could you come in for a moment?' she asked.

Anne shut her book and followed her sister into the kitchen.

'Did you hear the doorbell just now?' Margot asked. Anne shook her head. 'A notice arrived for Dad,' Margot continued softly. 'He has been called up for work camp.'

Shocked Anne looked at Margot. 'A work camp? That's terrible!'

'Don't worry, Anne. We'll stay together,' Margot almost whispered. 'We're going into hiding.'

'Into hiding? But where?'

'Mum and Dad will tell us shortly.'

Father was visiting an acquaintance in a special Jewish nursing home – *de Joodse Invalide*. It could be a while before he would return home.

'Where is Mum?'

'She has gone straight to the Van Pels family. They are coming with us. They have to talk things through.'

Anne's thoughts were all over the place. Mr and Mrs Van Pels and Peter were coming along? Going into hiding with seven people? How on earth were they going to manage that? Would they have to go to the countryside, would they be living with strangers in the middle of nowhere? What would happen to their things? What about the cat, Moortje? They were not allowed to travel anyhow, were they now? Would that mean a hiding place somewhere in the city? But where? And how would they get food?

'Come on,' Margot said, 'Mum said we should collect some things we want to take with us.'

'But, Margot...'

'I really don't know,' Margot answered as if she knew what was going on in Anne's head.

The doorbell. 'Hello! I forgot about him!' Anne realised.

'We can't let anyone in now,' Margot whispered.

Just then they heard the front door. Mother had returned with Mr Van Pels. They talked to Hello, but Anne couldn't hear what was being said. Probably something like: 'Now is not a good moment, Hello.' Once upstairs Mother didn't mention it. She just told Anne to continue packing.

Anne understood this was no time for asking questions. She returned to her room, picked up her school bag and filled it with everything she thought she might need in the hiding place. Her favourite fountain pen, given to her by Grandma Höllander, some pencils, a few precious letters, school books and of course her diary. While she busied herself trying to fit everything into her bag Margot entered the room. 'Anne, I have to tell you something,' she said gravely. 'The notice, it wasn't for Dad, it was meant for me. I have to report for work camp.'

'You?' Anne started to cry.

'Come on,' Margot said as calmly as she could. 'We have to continue packing. Tomorrow morning we'll leave. All of us.'

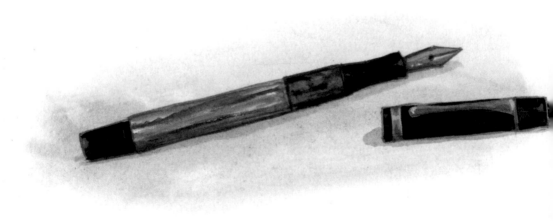

Father returned home at the end of the afternoon. People came and went. Mr Kleiman, one of Father's office staff, talked to Anne's parents. Miep also appeared to pick up some things, returning later in the evening with her husband Jan. They were wearing large rain coats, which was a little funny as it wasn't raining, but their purpose soon became clear: they had large, deep pockets. 'Give that to me,' Miep said to Mother, 'I can fit some more in here.' Underwear, clothes, socks all disappeared into those deep pockets. 'I'll make sure you get these things as soon as possible.' Only few words were spoken. All were worried and fearful. Everyone tried their hardest to stay calm and not to panic. It was almost midnight when Anne went to bed. Totally exhausted, she fell asleep almost immediately.

The next morning Mother woke her at 6.30am. There was still so much to do. Father explained to Anne and Margot what would happen. Miep and Margot would leave around 7.30am on their bicycles. It was best to get Margot to the hiding place sooner rather than later. Father, Mother and Anne would leave a little later on foot.

'Where are we going, Dad?' Anne asked.

'I'll tell you when it's time,' Father said.

Mother handed her a large pile of clothes. 'Put these on, Anne. All of them if you can. We don't know how long we will be staying away. We have to take as much as we can, as we cannot be seen carrying suitcases.'

'But...'

'Do as I ask, Anne.' The stern tone of Mother's voice made Anne do as she was asked immediately. Vests, trousers, a dress, a skirt, a jacket and another coat: one thing over the other. It was raining, but nevertheless it was pretty warm outside. Too hot to wear all these things.

Miep arrived on her bicycle at 7.30 on the dot. It was raining cats and dogs. Time for Margot to leave with Miep. Fearfully Margot looked at each of them. Eyes filled with so many questions: What if my parents and Anne are arrested on their way over? Or Miep? Or me? What if we will never see each other again?

'It is going to be alright,' Father spoke softly. 'We will see you later.'

Margot got on her bicycle. The Star of David had been taken off her coat. This was considered a criminal offence! Miep could also get into big trouble for helping a Jewish girl. Reasons enough to be very, very afraid. Still, they had to go.

Not much later Father, Mother and Anne were also ready to leave. Anne gave Moortje, her cat, one last cuddle. 'Goodbye sweet Moortje. I will miss you so much.' She looked at the note that Mother had left for the neighbours. They would look after Moortje, she was sure of that. Mother also added a note with an address in Maastricht. Anne's parents hoped the neighbours could be fooled into thinking they had fled to Switzerland via Maastricht. Then it was time to leave. They shut the door, went down the stairs and into the streets.

'We are going to my office, Anne,' Father said softly once they were on their way. 'There is a place there where we can hide.'

Anne looked at her father in surprise. 'At the office? But where?'

'You'll see. Mr Van Pels, Mr Kleiman, his brother and I

have been planning this for months and have been bringing things over. The intention was to go into hiding in ten days' time. It is not quite ready right now, but it will have to do.'

The walk from their apartment at the Merwerde Square to the office at the Prinsengracht took about an hour, but felt like an eternity. Carrying a bag each and wearing layers of clothing did not help either. And in the pouring rain.

'Walk as normal as you possibly can,' Father had said before leaving. 'Not too fast, not too slow. Keep your back straight and don't do anything that may look suspicious.'

Soaked to the bone they arrived at the 263 Prinsengracht, Father's office. Miep had already been on the look-out and quickly let them in. Father, Mother and Anne followed her through the building, through the corridors, up the stairs until they stopped in front of a grey door. Behind this door there were more stairs and at the top stood Margot. How happy they were to see her all safe and well!

Anne looked around in surprise. Things were piled on top of each other, higgledy-piggledy. Boxes, chairs and tables, beds, bed linen, cans of food, games, books. It looked like everything had just been shoved into the rooms. Nothing was in its rightful place. To be able to live here, a lot of work had to be done. But still, it was a home. A whole house behind that one grey door. Our Annexe, Anne thought.

'Anne and Margot', Father said. 'Come and sit with us for a moment.' They tried to find a spot to sit amongst all the boxes. 'Downstairs people are working. And we have to ensure the neighbours won't hear us. We have to whisper during the day and take off our shoes.'

They nodded.

'We have to be invisible. The first thing we will do is to put up black-out curtains. These will stay shut. *Always*. Is that clear?'

They nodded again.

'There are times during the day that the only place where people work is the store room. These people do not know we are here. This means at those times we cannot use the taps or flush the toilet. If they hear water running through the pipes, it might give us away.' They understood. 'When our helpers are in the building to work, using water and flushing the toilet is allowed, as staff in the store room will not pay particular attention at those times. Then, after all, more people are in the building and no-one would notice.' Anne, Margot and Mother looked at Father silently. 'It will be difficult,' he said. 'But we are together and that is all that counts.'

They would get help, Father continued. Miep, Mr Kugler and Mr Kleiman would get food and other things they may need. And also Father's employee Bep would help. All four of them had known for some time that the Frank family and the Van Pels family would go into hiding. Staff in the warehouse, however, did not know and it was best to keep it that way. The fewer people knew, the less the chance that they would be betrayed.

Mother and Margot listened to everything, but seemed paralysed with fear and tiredness. They looked for two empty beds to rest. But so much had to be organised. Father stood up and Anne followed him. The curtains needed to be hung, or at least something make-shift put up for now. Boxes had to be unpacked, floors scrubbed, beds to be made. They had

Miep

Mister Kleiman

to fix special black-out sheets for the evening and night. They got on with the job quietly. Very quietly.

And so the first days passed. Anne got to know the Annexe quite well. She had been here before, but now all the rooms had other purposes. It felt like a whole different place. When entering the Annexe through the grey door, the first thing you saw was a washbasin and a toilet to the right. Behind this washroom was the small room Anne and Margot shared and next to that was their parents' room. The rooms were connected by a door which Anne thought very comforting; this way she could always go to Pim if she was afraid at night. From her parents' room you could walk back to the entrance, making, as it were, a little circle.

Mister Kugler

Bep

Behind the grey door, a steep staircase went straight up to the first floor to the communal living room, which doubled as Mr and Mrs Van Pels' bedroom. This housed the kitchen area too. Peter had his own bed in a very tiny room just off the communal living room, where another staircase led to the attic where they would store their food.

It was comforting that Father had managed to bring over some things from their apartment over the past few months. These belongings made it a little bit more like home.

'Look,' Father said. 'This is what I brought especially for you.'

Anne recognised the box immediately. 'My collection of movie star photos and picture post cards! This is great!'

Armed with the box and a pot of glue, Anne went to her

room and began selecting her favourite pictures that she would stick to the walls. These decorations would surely brighten up the room. Every picture had a story attached to it. It was lovely to look at them and dream, to forget that awful war for just a moment. She thought of Hanneli, Jacqueline, Sanne and Hello. By now they would have discovered they had gone. When would she see them again?

Exactly a week after Anne and her family had arrived at the Annexe, the Van Pels family moved in. Mrs Van Pels even brought her own pot to pee in. They all thought that was terribly funny and it caused a lot of laughter. Days were filled with reading, studying, cooking, playing games, doing the laundry. Weeks turned into months.

In November of 1942 an eighth person arrived, a dentist named Mr Pfeffer. He was no stranger. Anne knew him too. Mr Pfeffer and his wife Charlotte used to visit the Frank family every once in a while on Saturday afternoons. Charlotte wasn't Jewish so she did not have to go into hiding. From then on, Margot slept in her parents' room and Anne became Mr Pfeffer's roommate.

The entrance to the Annexe was, by this time, no longer just a grey door, but a revolving book case. Mr Kugler's idea. 'This way the hiding place is totally invisible.' And it worked. The 'bookcase-door' was the unlikeliest entrance to a whole house anyone would expect!

Still, the space was very confined for eight frightened people, scared of discovery. This would sometimes lead to tension and arguments. Between the adults, but also between the adults and the children. Then again, Peter was too boring to do anything wrong, Anne thought, and Margot: well, she was almost a saint of course. She, herself, on the other hand...

'That daughter of yours has no manners,' Mrs Van Pels often muttered to Mother. And by 'that daughter' she meant Anne, always Anne.

'As if she is such a joy to be with,' Anne would counter upon hearing those comments. No, it wasn't always easy to stay calm and not to yell, stomp around, or slam the doors.

A good thing she had her diary in which she could vent all her anger, sadness, fear and frustration. If it wasn't for that...

The best times of the day were when one of the helpers would pop in. They always brought food, books, magazines and... news! 'Miep, what's it like outside?' Anne would ask. 'How's Jan? Do you have any news on my friends? Are they safe?' Anne had so many questions, but Miep and the other helpers could not always answer them.

For general news they listened to the radio. Radio Orange was broadcast from London, where the Queen and her government had sought refuge, giving people in occupied Holland the latest news on the war. Dutch radio and Dutch newspapers had to bring news that was approved by the Nazis. The people in hiding wanted to know what was really going on. And so they secretly listened to the prohibited broadcasts of Radio Orange. In the evening they would go downstairs and find a space in Father's old private office.

'Oh Pim, please let's go back upstairs again. Please, please,' Anne begged her father when they first went downstairs. The idea that they had left the safety of the Annexe to sit in the office where other people might hear them frightened her to bits. As time went on it became less scary. They all wanted to hear news that would tell them liberation was approaching. They just had to know, dangerous or not!

The most frightening moments were in the evening and at night. Anne was often scared, even more so than during daytime. She would recall the stories Mr Pfeffer had told about Jewish acquaintances who had been rounded up. The news on the radio that told of the murder of Jewish people.

And the rumours that the helpers had heard about camp Westerbork, where life for Jewish people was hell if stories could be believed. Anne was scared when noises of war and fights would enter the Annexe at night. She was afraid of guns, of the planes carrying bombs and that fire could break out if they were to be hit by one. She was afraid of break-ins and thieves who could discover that there were people hiding in the building. Afraid that someone would see a glimpse of light from one of the rooms and would betray them so that they too, would have to go to a camp. Afraid that something would happen to one of the helpers, preventing them from getting them more aid. Afraid that someone would get ill and no doctor would be able to come.

As ever when she was afraid, Anne would go in her pyjamas to her father, crying.

'Can I stay with you, Pim? Please?'

'Come here, girl.' If someone was able to soothe and calm her, it was her father.

Outside there was war. So they stayed inside. Day in, day out. Hidden away they quietly waited for this terrible war to end. They could hardly remember what it was like to open a front door and embrace the sunshine, the fresh air, to laugh out loud and walk the street, cross the road, ride a tram, do whatever you felt like doing. Outside had become the enemy. Outside was scary.

Still, one afternoon in July 1943 Mother said: 'I only see one solution.' She was referring to Anne's eyes, which had deteriorated. Reading and writing had become more difficult. 'Anne has to see an optician for a pair of glasses.'

'What?' Anne cried out.

'I know one nearby,' Miep said, 'a ten-minute walk away. If you want I can take her there.'

Anne felt hot and cold at the same time. 'But then I have to go outside!' Mother nodded. Miep looked grave. 'You are not serious are you, Mum? It is not possible is it? What if...'

'We're considering it, Anne', Mother said. 'We shall not make any hasty decisions.'

Getting out. Onto the street. For REAL! Anne and her family had already been indoors for a year now. A year and five days to be precise. Anne shivered at the thought of walking out of the door, feeling the wind on her face and in

her hair. Walking the streets of Amsterdam. Just being a girl taking a stroll.

She got her coat. She had had no need for it over the past year. But as she was putting her arms in the sleeves, she could feel it. Far too small. Everyone on the street would spot immediately she was not just a girl. She was a Jewish person in hiding. A person in hiding that had outgrown her coat.

'The Allied Forces are doing a great job,' Father said that same evening. 'With a bit of luck they are winning as we speak.' And then Anne knew. Pim would not send her to see an optician with Miep. It was far too dangerous. Just be patient a little longer. Perhaps the war would soon be over. **85**

Diary

Seasons changed. A second summer arrived at the Annexe.
Anne and her family, as well as the other people in hiding,
tried their best to keep their spirits up. It wasn't easy. There
wasn't a lot of space, everyone longed for peace and was
afraid of being discovered.

Now that they couldn't go outside, they were entirely
dependent on the help of Miep, Bep, Mr Kugler and Mr
Kleiman. Not only did they supply food, clothes and school
books, but those four also knew what was going on outside.
They brought newspapers and recounted what they had
heard and seen in the streets. Anne and the others assumed
the Nazis killed Jews in camps in Eastern Europe. The
helpers, however, did not tell every story they heard, as
those in hiding were scared enough already. They were
terribly afraid of being discovered and worried about family
and friends whose whereabouts they did not know.

Writing turned out to be Anne's escape from the
maddening fear and reality of the Annexe. She found it hard
to talk about the many things that filled her mind and heart.
Her diary became an imaginary friend: Kitty. She told Kitty

Writing turned out to be Anne's escape from the maddening fear and reality of the Annexe.

what happened in the Annexe. How the eight people in hiding were living together, day in, day out. She also wrote about her thoughts and dreams, a beautiful memory or a funny event. She would write everything down. She was just so glad to have her diary. Writing became her everything!

Anne's big dream

88 Whenever she closed her eyes she could still picture it in detail: the lovely spacious and airy room that she and Margot had shared in their apartment at Merwede Square. And Mother's lovely writing desk, with its tiny drawers and compartments. To Anne, that writing desk had probably been the most comfortable and nicest place in the house. Whenever Margot would visit friends or was busy in the living room, their room had been all hers. Wonderful. Nobody would disturb her writing notes and letters, and, particularly in the last weeks before going into hiding, making entries in the diary she had received for her birthday.

How different things were now; sharing a tiny, dark room with Mr Pfeffer. A man the same age as her father, who slept noisily and snored loudly in the bed next to hers. During the day he often sent her out of the room saying he required peace and quiet. As if she didn't want a bit of quiet just as much! How else was she supposed to work seriously on writing her diary? Her stories?

'Pim?' Anne said one afternoon in July 1943. 'You do know how important writing is to me, don't you?'

'Of course I do, Anne.'

'I would really love to have the private use of the little table in our room every once in a while. Have it to myself to write.'

'But can't you already use it every afternoon when Mr Pfeffer is having his nap?'

'Yes, but I would really like to have the room to *myself* a couple of afternoons a week.'

Father nodded his head. He understood. It was important to all of them to have some privacy now and again. To be away from quarrels, away from muttering and grumpiness, even away from the laughter, the whispers or all the general fuss.

'Perhaps it is best to discuss this with him yourself, Anne. After all, you share the room!'

And so Anne followed her father's advice later that day. Friendly and politely she asked: 'Mr Pfeffer, could I possibly have the room and the table to myself a couple of afternoons a week?'

'Certainly not.'

'What do you mean, Mr Pfeffer?'

'As I said, no.'

'But why not?' Anne asked, trying, at this point, her hardest not to get angry.

'I'm occupied with serious work. You are not. I need the table and the peace to work.'

A wave of anger engulfed Anne. She took a deep breath and slowly counted to ten as to not lose her temper. 'Surely we could share the table? I also need a place to work and study!'

But Mr Pfeffer ignored her. To him this conversation was over.

Anne was not one for giving up easily. That evening she

again tried to talk to Mr Pfeffer, but he became very agitated. 'Why does everything always have to be about you? You're such an annoying child!'

Clearly this wouldn't work. Father had to intervene and negotiate on Anne's behalf with Mr Pfeffer, who eventually succumbed after much fussing and grumbling. Anne would have private use of the table and sole use of the room two afternoons a week from 4pm to 5.30pm. Wonderful! An hour and a half of peace and quiet! Anne closed the door behind her. She filled her pen with ink and reached for the notebook she used for writing her stories. What shall I write today? Hmm. Let's write down how I acquired the sole use of this

table and the peace and quiet that comes with it. Not forgetting that childish Mr Pfeffer, who has not spoken to me since.

Anne put pen to paper and wrote: '*The best little table*'. She forgot the world around her. She wrote. And wrote. She considered every sentence. What she wanted to say and how. She tried to describe as accurately as possible what had happened, but made sure it would be interesting and fun to read. What did he call me again? '*Shamefully self-centred*'. Yes, that's what he'd said. And so Anne wrote that down. When her time was up she closed her notebook with satisfaction. If only I could become an author, she dreamt. A real famous one!

'Bep, you have to help me!'

Bep, just like the other helpers, would, whenever possible, come around at lunch time to see how they were doing and to ask if anything was needed at all. Sometimes she stayed for a bite to eat. She was barely on the stairs yet, when Anne jumped her.

'Let me guess,' said Bep, smiling, 'you're out of paper.'

'Oh, Bep, you have to find me something. Surely there is some paper around the office? Loose leaves for all I care, as long as it is something to write on.'

Bep smiled and shook her head. 'What in heaven's name are you writing down, Anne?'

'Everything!'

This was true. Whenever Anne had an argument with her mother, she wrote about it. When Mr Van Pels was preparing sausages, she couldn't wait to put the story on paper. When Mr Pfeffer had Mrs Van Pels in the dentist chair for a check-up, or when Father chuckled about something in a book by Charles Dickens, she would pick up her pen. To her diary she also entrusted her fears, her dreams and her thoughts on the books she'd read. About her slowly changing body developing from a girl into a young woman. And about stories they heard about life outside the Annexe.

Thus she wrote in her diary nearly every day. She also worked on imaginary stories. Yes worked, as to Anne writing was serious business. A real job. She really could do it all day, every day. Apart from reading a beautiful book, maybe. Or perhaps copying pretty sentences from those books into her 'Beautiful sentences book'. Or drawing up family trees. Another interest that required pen and paper. She cherished everything to do with reading and writing as if they were the greatest treasures in the world. Every evening she put her diary and stories away in an old briefcase Father had given her and placed it near his pillow for safekeeping. Father would look after her work and ensure it was safe. She could trust him.

But sometimes other things needed to be done. Learning algebra for example. Urgh. Or doing chores. On one such afternoon in November 1943, Anne picked up pen and paper to join Father and Margot at the living room table.

'No, Anne,' Father said. 'We need the table right now.'

'Latin.' Margot explained.

'What's more,' Mother, who was standing at the kitchen sink, said, 'I have a little chore you can do for me, Anne.' She handed Anne a small pot with beans. Yuck, they were all mouldy, Anne saw. 'Try to clean them one by one,' Mother said giving Anne a small cloth. 'We can't afford to throw them out.'

Anne muttered and put her papers and pen aside to make room for the filthy beans. While Father helped Margot with her Latin, Anne cleaned one bean after the other. When finished she swept up the dirt that had fallen on the floor and threw it in the fire. 'Finished!' she exclaimed.

'So are we,' Margot said.

'Well, then there is still some time for me to write a bit,' said Anne. She picked up her paper and reached for her fountain pen. It wasn't where she'd left it. Had it fallen to the floor? She crouched and looked into the darkness under the table trying to spot her pen.

'What are you looking for?' Margot asked.

'My fountain pen.'

'You didn't accidentally throw it into the fire with the filth of the beans, did you?'

'No, of course not!'

Mother joined the search. As did Father. And Peter and Mr Pfeffer. So did everyone. But Anne's fountain pen seemed to have disappeared.

When the ashes in the fireplace were closely examined the next morning, Anne saw something glisten. It turned out to be the golden tip of the fountain pen. So Margot had been right… Gone was that very special fountain pen she was given by Grandma Höllander when she was nine. The fountain pen she'd always taken to the Jewish grammar school and even to the Montessori school before that. The pen she had used every day since they had entered the Annexe. Gone. Anne had to swallow back a few tears.

But worse things happened. There was a lot of tension in the Annexe. Outside the safe walls of the hide-away people feared for their lives. The stories and tension deeply touched Anne, but she couldn't talk about it to anyone. It was too sad and too difficult. She could write about them, however, because she could trust Kitty. Kitty would never tell. And when she wrote she made sure nobody would disturb her or peek over her shoulder. The others sometimes asked her to read out what she had written. She would, occasionally, but only if she really wanted to herself. Being in the Annexe did not give her many options and choices. She had to obey her parents. The Nazis had taken away many liberties. But her papers and her thoughts would remain her own!

One Saturday in November 1943 Anne took a deep breath and wrote down what had happened to her the previous evening. When she had closed her eyes to go to sleep, she suddenly had a vision of Hanneli. Thinking about it now, it just upset her again. Anne took her pen and wrote: '*I keep seeing her enormous eyes, and they haunt me.*' Hanneli looked awful. She was skinny and her clothes were dirty and torn. She looked at Anne with a sad face. Anne had felt horrible picturing Hanneli like this. It made her feel guilty. She had abandoned her. There she was, lying in her warm bed in the Annexe, scared, but also safe. For now anyway, as nobody could predict how long this war would last. Father was here, as well as Mother and Margot. The food wasn't always tasty, but at least they had something to eat. Her clothes didn't fit her anymore, but they were in one piece and clean. But Hanneli, sweet Hanneli, could be somewhere in some dreadful camp. Hungry, cold, perhaps all on her own. There was nothing Anne could do. Not a thing. She could only think of her and pray. As she did for all her friends who might be in a camp far away. And so Anne prayed. For Hanneli, Jacqueline, Sanne and all the others. Many times and often.

The New Year arrived. But what did that mean when every day, every hour, you were imprisoned and afraid of being found? 'We have to keep faith!' the people in hiding would say to each other. 'We can't give up hope!'

Every evening they hoped for good tidings when they secretly listened to the radio. One evening in March 1944, Minister Bolkestein was speaking on Radio Orange. He was Minister of Education and, just like Queen Wilhelmina, had fled to London where the Dutch government was in exile.

'*If future generations want to know what happened during this war,*'

the Minister said, '*we would need simple accounts from ordinary people. A diary, letters from a person working in Germany, a series of speeches from a vicar or priest.*'

'He's talking about your diary!' Mrs Van Pels chuckled.

'Yes, Anne, if there is one person that writes a lot about our lives here, it is you,' Mr Van Pels added. Father patted her knee.

What if I could compile my notes and turn it into a novel, Anne later thought. A novel on the events and our life in the Annexe. Imagine: A real book! A book with my name on its cover!

The longer she thought about it, the more appealing the idea became. But Anne also had doubts. She obviously had to re-read all her previous notes. Some entries had to be left out. They were too personal. The sentences had to be better structured and more intelligent. Sometimes perhaps funnier and more creative. Then maybe this idea could work. Or not? For certain: she would love to become an author, more than anything, but could she do it?

Sometimes something happened that was so big, so overwhelming that it begged to be written down! Such a thing happened about a week after the radio speech of Minister Bolkestein. It was Easter Sunday and there was a break-in in the building. It had happened before and it always generated a lot of fear. This time however fear turned into horror. The burglars had had a fright and had fled when Father, Mr Van Pels, Mr Pfeffer and Peter went down the stairs. Father and the other men had then tried to mend the hole that the burglars had kicked in the storeroom doors. A couple that happened to be passing had heard the noise and had shone a torch inside.

Everyone in hiding went to the upstairs communal living room as quietly as they could. It seemed the couple had called the police. At least, that was what they assumed, as they could not check what was happening downstairs. But they heard people. No words could describe the fear of being found. But Anne tried a few days later. *'Footsteps in the house, the private office, the kitchen, then... on the staircase. All sounds of breathing stopped, eight hearts pounding. Footsteps on the stairs, then a rattling at the bookcase.'*

Here is where it ends, Anne had thought. Any moment now the door would open and Nazis would arrest them. It didn't happen though. Another shake of the bookcase, and another. But the door stayed closed. Receding footsteps. It all

went quiet. The people in hiding didn't dare to move a muscle. Everything was dark.

Because of it being Easter Sunday, it would be two days before there would be any staff in the office. As long as the helpers were out, the people in hiding did not know if the coast was clear.

'I have to use the bathroom,' Mr Van Pels said quietly.

'Not right now,' Father whispered.

'Here,' Peter said and handed his tin trashcan to his father, who didn't flinch. This was not a moment for embarrassment. One after the other they used the trashcan as a toilet. In disarray they all lay on the cold, hard floor but nobody dared to sleep.

'We have to hide the radio,' Mrs Van Pels whispered.

'If they find the radio, they will also find Anne's diaries,' Father said.

'Then we have to burn them,' Mrs Van Pels responded. 'That diary is just as dangerous. The Nazis won't like it one bit.'

Anne's heart missed a beat. Burn her work? Surely they were joking? But nobody moved. They were too paralysed with fear.

Anne later wrote how the situation was diverted. The police left without them being found. The people in hiding called Mr Kleiman, who in turn contacted Miep. She went to the Annexe with her husband Jan to tell them it was all clear. They were safe. For now.

After that night, however, fear had increased tenfold. They were all reminded once again that their lives had turned into a nightmare. That they were in hiding, locked in and hated. All because they were Jews. 'I have to be happy and thankful,' Anne whispered to herself. 'I cannot give up.'

She had to stay hopeful, otherwise all would be lost. Writing was a way to do this. She thought of Minister Bolkestein's appeal. Anne hesitated. Would her work be good enough for others to read?

On 20 May 1944 she finally made up her mind. She would do it. And she had to start straight away. The break-in had made it clear how vulnerable they all were. How long would they be safe?

Anne started her book. She had already thought of a title:

The Secret Annexe. First, she would re-write and edit her old entries and then compile them into one new story. She thought of the papers that were hanging to dry at the washing line in the attic of the Annexe. Such luck her diaries had not been on the table with the other papers yesterday when a vase with flowers had tipped over! She could see the fun of her homework on William of Orange and Charles v hanging to dry on clothes pegs. But her diaries... If they had been soaked, writing a book would have been out of the question!

'Go on, Anne,' she mumbled to herself, 'back to work.' She picked up a pile of loose papers Bep had given her, and started to write: *'Writing in a diary is a really strange experience for someone like me. Not only because I've never written anything before, but also because it seems to me that later on neither I nor anyone else*

will be interested in the musings of a thirteen-year-old schoolgirl.'

Yes, that was a good start, Anne thought. Obviously she hoped that it wouldn't be the case and that people would be interested in her work. That her stories would mean something to people. If she survived this terrible war, that would be the one thing she really wanted: to make a difference to people's lives. Not another face in the crowd, but someone who made the world a better place. By becoming a famous journalist.

Surviving

There did not seem to be an end in sight to the war. The people in hiding had a difficult time. They tried to lead as normal a life as was possible in the confined space of the Annexe with clear rules and chores. Anne, Margot and Peter did their homework. They celebrated national holidays and birthdays. But insecurity about the future saddened them. How long would they have to go on like this? What if the Nazis still found them after all this time? What if someone betrayed them? The fear was maddening. Still, they all looked for ways to keep their spirits up. They wanted to survive this war! Every now and then good news on the radio raised their hopes for a quick end to the war.

For Anne, contact with the helpers was key to perseverance. Everything they did for the people in hiding only proved to Anne that there were also good people in the world. Anne also was convinced that Grandma Höllander was looking out for her from heaven, like a guardian angel. For Mother and Mr Pfeffer, faith was an important source of strength. Anne did not think much of religion at first. Mother gave Anne her prayer book to read in the first months of

They tried to lead as normal a life as was possible in the confined space of the Annexe with clear rules and chores.

hiding but Anne wrote in her diary: '*They certainly sound beautiful, but they mean very little to me.*' Her faith in God, however, became more important during Anne's second year in the Annexe. The subject reappeared several times in her diary and her other stories. But Anne also found comfort and strength in other ways, by watching nature, for example.

103

Perseverance

'Mr Kleiman,' Anne said softly. She didn't want anyone else to hear.

Mr Kleiman was about to descend the stairs to return to the office. 'What's the matter, girl?'

'It is almost St Nicolas.'

Mr Kleiman nodded.

'I have an idea, will you help me?'

Mr Kleiman smiled at her. 'That depends, Anne. What's the idea?'

'I would like to give Bep and Miep a small St Nicolas present. You see, I saved some sugar over the past few months.' She handed Mr Kleiman a small paper bag. 'Every time I got some sugar for the porridge, I collected it in this bag. Now I would like to turn it into something sweet, so that I can give that to them as a present.'

Mr Kleiman looked kindly at Anne. 'That is very kind of you, Anne. Very sweet. I'll take it to the baker. I'm not sure if he can manage in time for St Nicolas. Would you mind if it would turn out to be a Christmas present instead?'

'That is fine too, Mr Kleiman. And this is our little secret?'

'My lips are sealed...'

Anne looked forward to surprising Miep and Bep with her small gift. The others would surely arrange something for Mr Kugler and Mr Kleiman. Where would they be if it weren't for the help of these friends? Anne knew that helping people in hiding was considered a criminal offence. The Nazis punished non-Jews who helped Jews severely. They would be sent to concentration camps or be executed. Still, the helpers never complained and did not show their worries to the people in hiding. They were the living proof that, besides those awful Nazis and the people that supported them, there were also many kind people around. People who couldn't care less whether you were Jewish or not.

But before Anne could surprise Miep and Bep, she and Margot received a present at Hanukkah, the Jewish festival of light, which also takes place in the month of December. This eight-day festival required the lighting of a candle in the menorah – a nine-armed candlestick – every evening. One candle every evening until they were all lit. With these lights the Jewish people celebrate the continuation of the Jewish faith. When all nine lights were lit, it was time for presents. 'A brooch! How beautiful!' Anne said after unwrapping her gift and Margot, too, was happy with her new piece of jewellery. Mr Pfeffer had asked Miep to bake a cake for Mother and Mrs Van Pels, so that also meant there was something sweet to enjoy. That must have been quite a feat for Miep, Anne thought. Just finding the ingredients would have been difficult. Most groceries were rationed and only available with food stamps. Things that were hard to get, like butter and sugar, were very, very expensive.

Christmas came around. This Christian feast would not normally be celebrated by Jewish people, but now they looked forward to a pleasant evening together. Not to mention that their helpers joined them on Christmas Eve. Everyone gathered around the table in the communal living room upstairs.

'A present!' Bep said. 'From all of us!' and she handed Peter, Margot and Anne a small parcel which they carefully unwrapped.

'A bottle of yoghurt! Thanks so much!' Anne exclaimed.

The adults too received a present. They carefully opened it and then smiled happily. A bottle of beer each. How they would enjoy that! Bep conjured up another gift: delicious butter biscuits, enough for everyone. Then, finally, Miep and Bep were presented with their gifts: the sweets. What a surprise. Mr Kleiman winked at Anne. She beamed. Miep came out with the finale – a home-made cake with the words *Peace 1944* written on top. Everyone was moved. How they wished this to come true. 1944, the end of the war. Peace. Oh how they longed for peace!

The New Year arrived. Not that the people in hiding noticed. Every day was like every other. Moments of peace and quiet to do some writing had become very important to Anne.

'Do not disturb!' Anne closed the door of her and Mr Pfeffer's room behind her and sat down at the little writing desk. She had finished her homework, and she had done the dishes and peeled the potatoes. Now there was time to write. Lovely! She lifted the large, sturdy notebook from her father's briefcase. '*Stories and events from the Annexe by Anne Frank*', the title said. She picked up her pen, leafed through to the first clean page and wrote with elegant letters: '22 February 1944. Tuesday'.

For a moment she closed her eyes and thought of a dream she had had about Grandma Höllander, almost two months ago. Grandma had died when Anne was twelve and she missed her every day. In this dream Grandma came back to life and ever since, she had felt her presence around her. Like a guardian angel who was looking out for her. Anne felt less lonely because of it.

She would write a story about that, she decided. The main characters would be another girl and her grandmother. She started to write. 'Once upon a time there were two people, an old woman and her granddaughter, who lived for many years at the edge of a great big forest.' Anne looked at her first sentence. Not bad. Let me think. What happens to the girl and her grandmother? Hmm. Grandma is falling ill. No, no. She dies. Yes, that's it: Grandma dies and her granddaughter, only fourteen years of age, is left behind without any other family, friends or neighbours.

What do you do when you are fourteen and you suddenly find yourself all alone? What would she do? Anne wrote: 'She lay down on her bed and wept.' Exactly. That's what you did when your grandmother suddenly died. She wasn't crying for one day, but every day for four whole weeks. Then something happened. One night, when the girl was asleep, her grandmother appeared at her bedside. Anne could see the picture in her head.

She put down her pen. What would the grandmother say to the girl? What would Grandma tell her, Anne? Anne knew. Keep your spirits up, girl! Come on: persevere! You have to look after yourself. You don't have to do it alone.

Now Anne continued writing. As neatly as she could she wrote: '*You mustn't think that I'll stop looking after you now that I'm dead. I'm in Heaven, watching you from up above.*'

That must be an enormous comfort for the girl, Anne thought. Just like Grandma Holländer had always been there for her. Anne looked at her story with satisfaction. It was so exhilarating to have pen and paper and to express her thoughts and feelings in this way. She used to want to excel in drawing, but found she couldn't do it. She didn't mind anymore, because she could write. Her writing was probably the most wonderful skill she possessed.

One day Bep visited to get the grocery list and to catch up. She also stayed for lunch.

'Finished!' Anne pushed her soup bowl away from her. Another lunch finished. She could do with a bit more, and it would be great if it would be tasty for a change, but she did not complain. Now that the war in The Netherlands had been going on for four years, almost everyone had too little, too boring or just plain disgusting food. Not to mention that Bep and Miep were trying their utmost to find food for all of them. That was something to be very grateful for indeed.

'Please collect the plates, Peter,' Mrs Van Pels said. Peter stacked the plates and put them on the kitchen counter. Mother was already preparing soapy water for the dishes. Bep and Mrs Van Pels both reached for a tea towel. Anne sat herself down at the table and opened a book.

'You look tired, Bep,' she overheard her mother say. 'Are you okay?'

'It is not always easy,' Bep whispered softly, but loud enough for Anne to hear.

'Your father?' Mother asked. Bep's father was very ill, Anne knew.

'There is that too,' Bep sighed.

Mother put a comforting hand on Bep's arm.

'The war,' Bep said, her voice trembling. 'Sometimes I wonder if it is ever going to end.'

'Me too, Bep, me too,' Mrs Van Pels sighed.

'What if we don't make it?' Bep sounded like she was about to cry.

'Oh, Bep,' Mother said. 'We are not so badly off compared to other people.'

Anne jumped up. 'How can you say such a thing, Mother!

What good is it to Bep if you comfort her by saying that others are worse off? Is that going to help?'

'Anne, this is *not* a conversation for a child.'

'But Mum, do you really think…'

'I'm warning you, Anne,' Mother snapped.

But Anne hadn't finished yet. She went over to Bep. 'You know, Bep…' she started.

But now Father, who had followed the whole conversation from a corner of the room, stood up. He pushed Anne towards the door. 'Enough, Anne,' he said with a stern voice. 'Go to your room.'

Anne felt like she was slapped across the face. Mother and Mrs Van Pels being stupid wasn't new to her, but Father not giving her a chance to speak her mind… that hurt. While she walked to her room she felt tears burn in her eyes. She had so much wanted to share what she had recently discovered. She had noticed that it was possible to be really happy even if there was a war outside and you were frightened. She knew now that happiness could be found deep inside, in your heart. You didn't need anyone else to be happy. And nobody could take that inner happiness away. Not even those horrible Nazis. When she looked at the birds, the flowers and all the beautiful things around her she felt happy. Really happy! But she was prevented from saying this. Mother got angry and Father had sent her to her room.

Looking at nature was a way to comfort herself, Anne had learned. Still, she longed for someone with whom to share her thoughts. Could she talk to Peter? Anne often wondered. She knew for sure she would go mad if she wasn't able to share her thoughts with Kitty in her diary. Kitty was like a dear friend. And Grandma's presence, which Anne felt so strongly, was a great comfort too. But how she longed to talk to someone. Someone who would talk back. Could this someone be Peter?

Anne increasingly spent the mornings in the attic. During office hours it was the only window that would be ajar. To get there, she had to pass through Peter's room. This is where the stairs to the attic were located. One morning, at the end of February 1944, Anne climbed up the steep stairs. She sat down on her favourite spot and took a deep breath of fresh air. A moment later Peter sat down beside her. Together they looked out at the blue sky. Anne enjoyed those quiet minutes together. The sun was out and everything outside looked pretty and peaceful. Anne longed to talk to Peter. Really talk. She wanted to share her feelings with him and for him to share his thoughts and feelings with her. Not at this moment though. The silence felt comfortable.

God has created nature in all its splendour with good reason, Anne thought. He made it the way it is because he wants us humans to enjoy it. Feel that happiness so deep in our souls, where nobody can take it away! One day we will be liberated and free to go outside. Until that time comes, God will comfort us by letting the flowers bloom and the sun shine. She had hardly ever really thought about God before. But now she was certain. God was with her, just like Grandma.

'Not that much!' Mother cried out. It had turned summer; the summer of 1944. The people in hiding had spent two years in the Annexe. They were short of everything, which resulted in heated discussions.

'I have just as much right to a little bit of butter as everyone else in this house,' Mr Pfeffer stubbornly said.

'Exactly. Just as much right. As much, not meaning "more"!'

'I don't have more!'

'Yes you do. I'm looking at it?!'

Mother angry, Father grumpy, Mr Pfeffer unbearable, Mrs Van Pels ill. Mrs Van Pels... she was always in a bad mood. '*If only we could plonk her down in the loft in a bucket of cold water!*' Anne wrote. Outside it rained. Even the cat living in the warehouse was not its usual self: she slept in the cat litter and pooped and urinated in the wrapping material. In short: how much more pleasant could it get? Anne thought ironically.

The worst was that their funds were depleting. She sighed. Where could they get money for the shopping that the helpers were trying to get? If only there was some good news.

The good news came as soon as the next day. A radio broadcast: 'D-Day has come.' They looked at each other in surprise. Did they hear this right? Had the Allied Forces landed in occupied France? Would they slowly chase the Nazis out of the other countries they had so violently taken? Would thet beat Nazi-Germany?

'There will be much fighting to come,' they heard American General Eisenhower say on the radio. He led the Allied Forces into battle so he would know. 'But after that there will be victory,' he continued. '1944 will be the year of complete victory.'

This was fantastic news! The best news they had heard for ages! They hardly dared to believe it.

'Perhaps we can even return to school after summer,' Margot mused.

'What a nice thought that there are foreign friends on their way to help us,' said Anne, beaming.

Infatuation

That only left one person with whom she might be able to share her thoughts. Peter.

In January 1944 Anne had been living in the Annexe for a year and a half. She missed her friends. It was impossible to contact them, as this would put them and the helpers in severe danger.

There were only two other young people in the Annexe, Margot and Peter. But both had a few years on Anne. Margot and she were too different to be anything but sisters, let alone friends even though their bond had strengthened during their time in the Annexe. Kitty, her diary friend, although treasured, was not a human being of flesh and blood. She could not talk back. This was something Anne really needed.

That only left one person with whom she might be able to share her thoughts. Peter. Peter who turned out to be quite a nice boy. Boy? Almost a man really.

Attic kisses

'A colourful prince,' Anne heard Peter mumble as she entered his room. He was engrossed in a small pocket book with crossword puzzles, sitting at the small table in his room. Anne sat herself down on the bed next to the table. 'What's the subject of the clues?' she asked.

'Historical figures.'

'Brilliant! I'm good at those. How many letters?'

'Many.' Peter counted the squares with his finger. 'One, two, three... thirteen, fourteen, fifteen. Fifteen letters.'

'Colourful prince!' Anne jumped enthusiastically from the bed. 'I know!'

Peter looked at her in surprise. 'Really?'

'William of Orange!' she answered. 'Count the letters.' She held up her fingers. 'W-i-l-l-i-a-m is seven, o-f is two and O-r-a-n-g-e is six. So seven plus two plus six makes fifteen.'

Peter looked at the squares. The third square already had an 'l' and the second but last contained a 'g'. It was right, Anne was right.

'Thank you,' Peter said. He gave her a friendly, but shy smile. Anne felt a small butterfly in her stomach when she looked into his dark blue eyes. She'd never really noticed, but he was really quite a handsome boy. Then again, boy? A man almost. Peter was already seventeen.

Anne looked around. Peter's small room really was kind of cosy. Just like in her room, he had stuck some pictures of movie stars to the walls. She had given those to him. He'd also nailed four crates that had contained potatoes to the wall, but were now lined with his books. The stairs to the attic were in the middle of the room and behind it he had hung his bicycle, which he hoped to use again one day soon.

Anne wouldn't mind being in Peter's room more often. But she wouldn't dare to just barge in. If she could think of a good excuse to come and visit, it would be so much easier. She had seen her chance earlier that day when Peter mentioned he was going to do a crossword puzzle. She had

asked if she could help. And so here they were.

But really Anne wanted more than just doing a crossword. I would really like to talk to someone, she thought. Not just a bit of chit-chat or talking about crosswords, but about real things. Important things. How she felt and what she thought.

Later that night in the silence of her own room, she thought of Peter. How she longed for friendship! With a boy or a girl, that didn't matter. She was just looking for someone who would understand her. Hiding in the Annexe, she missed her friends terribly. Now that she had spent time with Peter and had looked into his shy eyes, the longing for her friends had become even stronger. Could Peter be a real friend? After all, he must feel just as lonely as she did. Lonely, lonely, all alone. The words echoed in her head. Anne cried. She buried herself under the blankets and tried to suppress her sobs so nobody would hear. Eventually she fell asleep.

That night she dreamt of Peter. But not Peter van Pels. It was Peter Schiff who appeared in her dreams, the boy she had had a major crush on a few years previously. He had fancied her too. Just like her, Peter had moved to Holland from Germany to escape the Nazis. One long summer they had been inseparable. Then he started secondary school while she was still at primary school. He had become a bit distant after that. Being three years older meant he became more interested in girls his own age. Petel, she had always lovingly called him. She would never forget him.

In her dream she and Petel were looking at a book of drawings together. It was lovely to be that close to him! And he must have liked it too, because he looked into her eyes and put his cheek softly to hers. And then... Anne woke up.

Petel! Anne touched her cheek. She could still feel his soft, cool cheek to hers. He was so near. She had last seen him in front of the Blankevoort bookshop near their apartment at Merwede Square just before going into hiding. They had just greeted one another. But now she could clearly picture him again. That intelligent, tall and slender boy with the velvety brown eyes. It was lovely and sad at the same time. I'm still in love with Petel, Anne thought with a little shock. He's the one for me!

In the days that followed, Petel was never far from her mind. She still missed someone to share her thoughts with in the Annexe. But she felt a little less lonely. The lovely memories of Petel somehow seemed to keep her going. He wasn't with her in person, but she could still pretend to be talking to him. Just by thinking of him.

'Dear God,' she prayed, 'if we ever leave the Annexe, will you let me find Petel again?'

Nevertheless Anne still hoped that she and Peter van Pels would become friends. That would perhaps improve life in the Annexe a little. So in the following weeks she tried her best to get closer to him. Still, it was hard to figure out what his thoughts were on this. Did he appreciate that she tried to talk to him more often? Did he like her at all, for that matter? Perhaps he didn't need attention and friendship? Hard to believe though, as everybody needed someone, didn't they? Sometimes he gave her a friendly smile that made Anne all warm inside. But he didn't really talk. She wanted to become friends so much that for weeks it was almost the only thing on her mind.

It was a Saturday evening in March 1944 when Anne found Peter at the open window of his room. Peter was so lucky: his window wasn't visible to the neighbours. If they were careful and quiet, they could sometimes open it.

'Can I come in?' she asked.

'Sure.'

She went over to the other side of the window. 'Are you okay?'

'I guess. You?'

'Well enough,' Anne said. 'I'm just glad my parents and I have stopped bickering.'

'Your family doesn't have that many arguments though, do they?'

'We didn't used to. But Father and Mother still sometimes treat Margot and me as the little children we no longer are. This is rather irritating.'

Peter nodded and stared ahead.

'So, that's what we argue about.'

They were silent for a moment.

'Everyone has changed quite a bit since we live here, don't you think?' Peter noted.

Anne started to chuckle. 'Well, I think you have become a lot nicer,' she said. 'I really thought you were quite a bore in the beginning.'

'And I thought you were noisy and difficult.'

They both laughed.

'I've changed my mind though,' Anne said quietly. 'I am very happy you are here now.'

'And I'm happy you are here!' Peter said spontaneously.

Anne beamed. 'Really?' she asked carefully.

Peter nodded his head. Anne felt herself blushing. How

sweet! This meant they now could really talk to each other about the things on their mind and their feelings.

'*The most wonderful evening I've ever had in the Annexe,*' she happily wrote in her diary.

From that moment on Anne and Peter spent more time together. Anne came to Peter's room or they went to the attic, a place where they could be together without being seen or being overheard. They talked often now. Sometimes they sat quietly enjoying the birds, the sky and the chestnut tree outside as it slowly started to bloom.

Was she imagining it or was Margot looking a bit sad when she and Peter would leave to go to the attic? Would Margot... no, surely not, or would she? After some reflection Anne just had to ask her sister. 'Margot, I really like being in Peter's company. You don't mind, do you?'

'No, Anne. Of course not.'

'Are you sure?'

Margot nodded her head. 'It's fine.'

But the next morning Anne found a letter from Margot on her pillow. She opened it eagerly. Her eyes followed Margot's neat handwriting. Margot wrote that she did mind. Not because she was in love with Peter, but because she herself was also longing for someone to share her thoughts and feelings with. She was happy for Anne though, as she seemed to have found that with Peter.

Anne felt a lump in her throat. What a sweet letter. How she admired her sister. And she would tell her so straight away. She sat down at the writing desk and wrote a response. To this Margot answered again. It was very special to Anne that she and Margot slowly started to have a better understanding of each other.

Spring 1944. Anne still thought of Petel. But now she also wondered whether or not she might be falling in love with Peter. She really adored him now. But did he feel the same? Would she ever feel his cheek to hers, as she had felt Petel's cheek in her dream? Sometimes Peter put an arm around her and played with one of her curls. But that was all.

Until that one Saturday night in April 1944. It was around eight in the evening when Anne sat with Peter on his bed. Anne noticed Peter moving closer to her, closer than they had ever physically been. Anne carefully put her head on Peter's shoulder. He in return put his chin on her head. Thus they sat quietly. Peter caressed Anne's cheek and arm and stroked her hair. She felt so happy!

But after half an hour it was time to leave. They both got up and before Anne realised what was happening, Peter kissed her. Her first kiss! *'Remember yesterday's date,'* she wrote in her diary the following day, *'since it was a red-letter day for me.'*

In love after all! Now what? The others were already joking about their get-togethers in the attic. Weeks earlier her mother had already tried to stop her from being alone with Peter. According to Mother, Anne's friendship with Peter was making Mrs Van Pels jealous and it was not a good idea to spend so much time alone together. Mrs Van Pels would only get irritated. What if it caused arguments and discussions? They really could do without those in the Annexe, so she had said. Anne didn't know what to think. Was Mother serious? Or did she just not want her to be with Peter? They decided they really couldn't care less. Even the jokes didn't bother them. But now it had come to this kiss. Was it time to be honest? Father probably wouldn't approve. But was she really bothered? For almost two years now they had lived each day in fear and worry. Surely the nicest thing in these circumstances was to find comfort with each other?

Anne decided to talk to Father about Peter. She told him about their conversations, but also about their cuddles in the attic. Father looked worried. He advised her that it might be better not to spend so much time together. He was afraid she might be disappointed. *'Be careful, Anne, and don't take it too seriously!'* he said. Anne wrote those words in her diary, but to her it was simple: she would be going to Peter and Father just had to trust her. She enjoyed the cuddles, the kisses and being together in the attic. Anne had finally found what she had longed for ever since entering the Annexe: friendship. It was lovely. But... a little voice was nagging her. Peter was

sweet for sure. A genuine friendly and warm boy who was always happy to see her. But...

Anne looked at her notebooks and papers in the old briefcase. Her 'Beautiful Sentences'-book was filling up nicely. And her book *Stories, and events from the Annexe by Anne Frank* was also coming along. Not to mention her diary and *The Secret Annexe*. When writing, she could really be herself. She could pen down all her thoughts. On paper she could be cheerful, scared, enthusiastic, grumpy. Everything. But could she also be herself with Peter? Did he really, really understand what she was about? He had said he'd loved her cheerfulness. But did he also see her other side? In her diary and stories she could write about God, about nature, about her body, which was slowly developing from that of a girl into a young woman's. She could express how she longed for peace, but also about the strength she had found which made the terror and violence of war a bit easier to bear. She had really gotten to know herself in the past few years!

But could she speak to Peter about all these things? If you are really honest with yourself, Anne, you know that this is not the case, she told herself. If Peter was thinking about all these difficult subjects, then he didn't show it. He wasn't much of a talker. And really, he didn't ask many questions either. Asking more leading questions and thus deepening their conversations was not something he did.

A month had gone by since that first kiss in April and Anne could no longer deny her doubts. She was disappointed in Peter. She really had thought things would change: that they would slowly confide in each other more. It hadn't happened. He didn't turn out to be that wonderful friend she had been longing for. They were just too different. It was as simple as that.

Anne did notice, however, that she was very important to Peter. This felt good. It was nice, very nice, that someone in the Annexe was so happy to be with her.

Betrayal

From July 1942 Jewish people had to report for work camps in Nazi Germany. Because not all Jews responded to this call-up, the Nazis began to hold round-ups. Round-ups were large and well-organised searches. A neighbourhood or street would be closed and houses individually searched. During these actions, Nazis literally dragged Jewish men, women and children from their homes and actively looked for possible hiding places. During the two years that the people were in hiding in the Annexe, more than one hundred thousand Jews were arrested during these round-ups in The Netherlands.

September 1943 saw the last big round-up. But there were still Jewish people in hiding, all of whom the Nazis also wanted to arrest. They offered attractive rewards if people told them or wrote to them where people were hidden. There were traitors who made a lot of money this way. These 'Jew Hunters' did their utmost to find Jews in hiding.

Once arrested, Jewish people were transported to Westerbork, a transition camp in the Netherlands. From

During the two years that they were
in hiding in the Annexe, more than one
hundred thousand Jews were arrested
during round-ups in The Netherlands.

there they were deported to camps in Eastern Europe. At
Westerbork, Jews that had been in hiding were separated
from others and taken to special punishment sheds. After all,
they had ignored the call-up to report voluntarily. They were
therefore also treated worse than the other prisoners.

Nazis at the Annexe

Okay. What was the best way forward? Anne removed her diary and the notebooks from her father's briefcase and put them in order on her bed. It was a lot. It would certainly keep her occupied this spring, the spring of 1944. She looked at her notebook with stories, her book with beautiful sentences and her diary entries. Two years of thoughts on paper. She had now decided to make these into a real book which she could perhaps publish after the war. A big job.

Anne had only just started re-organising her notes when, one afternoon a few days later, Miep entered the Annexe looking worried. 'Van Hoeve has been arrested,' she said. Van Hoeve was the greengrocer where Miep bought vegetables for the people in hiding. He was a man who sometimes, when storeroom staff were having their lunch break, would deliver large sacks of potatoes. 'He was hiding two Jews,' Miep explained. 'Somebody must have given him away.'

'Oh no!' Anne said in shock. 'Not just for the Jewish people, but for him as well.'

'His wife was terribly upset,' Miep continued. 'I spoke with her briefly. It all happened this morning.'

Nobody in the room dared to say it out loud, but what would become of them now? It was already a considerable feat for Miep and Bep to scrape together food for eight people in hiding. These kinds of events shook everyone to the bone. It is incomprehensible, Anne thought later, that people who help others are arrested and punished, while those who harm others are in charge.

Fortunately, other things happened that gave new hope. Two weeks after Van Hoeve's arrest, they heard that the Allied Forces had set foot on French soil. This day was known as D-Day. From Normandy, they intended to liberate the occupied countries in Europe and beat Nazi Germany.

'Look, Anne,' Father said. He showed Anne a map of Normandy he had pinned to the bedroom wall. His finger traced the map to a red pin he had stuck on a coastal town in northern France. 'This is Bayeux. They are already past that point. They are now fighting for Caen.' He sighed. 'They have the first one hundred kilometres behind them. The Russians are moving in from the other side. We have to be patient, Anne.'

Anne looked happily at her father. Still, inside her fear continued to overrule her feelings of hope. What if this war continued for years to come? What if peace never came? And what would happen if someone betrayed them? These were questions that had her worried every day. She shook her head while she looked at her diary notes. *No, no and another no.* She had to overcome her fear. She had to concentrate on the good things around her and write them down. This would be the only way to keep going.

It was August at the Annexe. Friday the 4th of August was a day just like any other. The clock said 10.30am. Anne saw her father accompanying Peter to his room for his English lessons. That morning at breakfast Father had promised him some dictation exercises.

'Be afraid, be *very* afraid, my boy!' Anne had piped up.

'Tease!' Peter had responded. But he was smiling.

Anne herself went to the room she had shared with Mr Pfeffer for so many months. Suddenly she heard an unfamiliar sound. Then she realised. Voices. My God, people were standing in front of the bookcase. Paralysed with fear she sat down on her bed. Then she heard the bookcase move. Footsteps and voices. They were entering the Annexe! 'You first,' she heard a strange man say in German.

And she knew immediately. They had been betrayed. It was over.

She didn't move a muscle. 'Where are the others?' she heard another man say insistently in Dutch. *Mother! Margot! They were in the room next door!* But Anne didn't hear their response.

'You, upstairs,' the German man ordered. Who was he talking to? Anne heard heavy boots going up the stairs to the floor where the Van Pels family lived. Then the door to her room opened. 'You, get in here,' the Dutch man said rudely.

Anne entered the room of her parents and saw her mother and Margot with their hands raised above their heads. A man was pointing a gun at her. 'Stand next to them.' Anne did as the man asked. Now she heard footsteps coming down. Mr and Mrs Van Pels and Mr Pfeffer entered the room, behind them a second man with a gun. Mr Kugler had also joined them.

Then down came Father and Peter, also with a gun to their backs. Here they all were. All nine of them with their hands up, threatened by three men with guns, including two Dutch policemen in civilian clothes. Margot wept quietly. The rest were silent. Anne too. This is what they had feared every day for the last two years. There was nothing more to say.

The German officer, the only one in military uniform, was in charge. 'Any valuables?' he sternly asked Father. 'Money? Jewellery?'

Father pointed at a small chest that was placed on the wall cabinet above Mother's bed. The German took the chest and looked inside. Then his eyes scanned the rest of the room. He looked at Father's bed to where his briefcase stood. He took two steps, grabbed the bag, ripped it open and looked inside. Paper. Nothing but paper. He turned it upside down and stuffed it with the valuables Father had handed him. Anne's diary, the notebooks and all the loose leaves fell to the floor. Anne was paralysed with fear. Her notes! Imagine them reading those! The helpers! And all other people mentioned in them!

'Five minutes,' the officer growled. 'You have five minutes to pack some things together. Then you assemble again in this room.'

The armed men dispersed over the two floors and watched them pack their bag packs with the most important things. They also rummaged through cupboards and drawers looking for valuables. Jewellery, money, documents. Things of no value to them were thrown on the floor. They made a terrible mess.

'A map of Normandy,' Anne heard the German say. He stood in front of Father's map on which he had marked all the places where the Allied Forces had defeated the German enemy. 'How long have you been hiding here?' he asked.

'Over two years,' Father answered.

'I don't believe it,' the German said.

'Look, here is where we mark how tall our children are,' Father said. They were near to Anne's room now. 'Look at the

marks and dates. That's how much my daughters have grown since we came here.'

When everyone had finished packing, they were ordered downstairs. Anne walked through her parent's room where her diary and all her papers were strewn over the floor. They were taken to Father's private office. There they also found their helpers Mr Kugler and Mr Kleiman.

'Did you know of this?' The German sternly asked Mr Kleiman. The other men were still holding their weapons at gunpoint.

'I have nothing to say,' Mr Kleiman said.

'And you?' he addressed Mr Kugler.

'I have nothing to say,' he also answered.

'Fine. In that case we will take you too,' the Nazi concluded.

After that they were all sent downstairs. They descended the stairs passing the office where possibly Miep and Bep were still being held. Or were they arrested? They didn't know. Anne saw the open front door. The sun was shining. It was a lovely summer's day. But they were in a nightmare. She stepped outside. The bright light hurt her eyes. For a few seconds she felt the warm wind on her face, her arms and her legs. A small truck was parked straight in front of the door. Once more she stepped into a dark and closed environment. On her way to... Well, to what? Her heart was beating fast. Anne had heard enough about the camps to be very afraid.

With her own family, the Van Pels family, Mr Pfeffer, Mr Kleiman and Mr Kugler she sat quietly in the truck. It wasn't a long ride. The truck stopped at a school building near their home at Merwede Square. They were ordered out. It was now

a Nazi office and prison. That much was clear from the large Nazi flag that hung outside.

They were taken to a room. Mr Kugler and Mr Kleiman were separated from them not much later. They waved at each other. They never saw each other again. The eight people who had been in hiding were taken to a prison cell in the basement of the building.

'What will they do to us, Dad?' Anne asked fearfully.

But Father didn't know.

'What about Mr Kugler and Mr Kleiman?'

Father again shook his head. They all feared the worst. Helping people in hiding was, after all, considered a crime.

The next day they were transferred to an Amsterdam prison. They stayed there for another three days and nights. In the early morning of August 8, Anne, Margot, their parents and the other people in hiding, along with many other prisoners, were taken to the main railway station of Amsterdam. 'Tomorrow you will leave for Westerbork,' they had been told the previous evening. 'There you will be put to work.' What kind of work they were required to do, they didn't know.

Anne stayed close to her parents and Margot that morning. The station was full of men with guns. A train was ready. A regular one. They had to get on.

Slowly the train was leaving the platform. Anne sat at the window and looked outside. She saw buildings, water, the sky, birds. She saw meadows as far as the eye could see, filled with cows and sheep. She saw flowers, trees in full glory green, roads and bridges. After two years in the dark and stifling Annexe, she, despite everything, enjoyed the sun, the

light and all the colours. Eventually the train slowed down and came to a halt.

Before them an enormous bare area opened up. As far as she could see, she saw large, green wooden sheds. Row after row of similar sheds, nothing in between. No trees, just a lot of bare earth and here and there a small patch of purple blooming heather. There were watchtowers occupied by men wearing helmets and carrying guns.

They were taken to a shed. 'S,' said an armed escort to a woman behind a typewriter. 'S'? What did that mean?

Forms were filled out. It took a long time. Then Mother, Margot, Anne and Mrs Van Pels were ordered to come along. In the meantime Father, Peter, Mr Van Pels and Mr Pfeffer were taken in the other direction. 'Be brave,' Father managed to whisper. But Anne worried. They followed a guard to a room where they had to hand in their belongings and were ordered to take off their clothes, everything but their underwear. Anne numbly did as she was told. Her clothes were taken away.

'Lice control!' they heard. 'This way!'

Then Anne noticed the scissors on the table and got really scared. My hair, not my hair, she prayed in silence. But a woman took her lovely locks and started to cut them off. Lock after lock fell to the floor. Anne felt tears burning. Mother, Margot and Mrs Van Pels were also cropped until there was nothing left but a few millimetres of hair. They then were given blue overalls to wear. Red patches were sewn on the shoulders and a Star of David on the chest. Wooden clogs replaced their shoes, hurting their bare feet. The state of them! Anne didn't know whether to laugh or cry.

'Come along!' someone ordered. They walked to the camp

area. The number of identical sheds seemed endless. They had to protect their eyes from the dust blown up by the wind. Strangely enough though, all people that Anne encountered on their way were wearing normal clothes. Their hair was not cut either. She looked questioningly at Mother. But Mother looked silently ahead.

The sheds that they were taken to were similar to all the others. The difference though was that they were separated from the others by a fence of barbed wire. It resembled a prison within this prison camp.

'The punishment sheds,' the escort said. 'That's where you will be taken. Shed 67.'

'And our men?' Mother asked.

'They will be staying in the men's part. You will see them tonight.'

Once inside they could not believe their eyes. The enormous space contained at least a hundred bunk beds. Not the usual double-bunks, but three beds on top of each other. In between ropes were hung, containing underwear and nappies drying. There were also wooden tables and benches. The women in the punishment shed all wore the same blue overalls with red shoulder patches. And everyone had hair cropped very short.

That night Anne gave her father a big hug. The little hair he had left was now shaven off. Peter, as well as the other men, were all bald. As well as the same blue overalls, they were also made to wear a funny blue and red cap. Father explained they were treated as punishment cases because they had been in hiding. The Dutch word for 'punishment' is 'straf', which explained the 'S' that was noted to the woman with the typewriter. They were not allowed to be with the other prisoners that had come to Westerbork. The overalls and haircuts would make them stand out and recognisable as such. On top of that, they would be made to work harder. But at least they would be allowed to see each other after work. That people in the punishment sheds were the first ones to be transported to the camps in the east of Europe, Father didn't dare to mention.

'We have to keep our spirits up!' he said. 'The Allied Forces are closing in. Let's do what they ask of us. That way we will manage here until the war is over, okay?'

And so Anne didn't complain when they were woken the next morning, and every morning thereafter, to go to work. She, Mother, Margot and Mrs Van Pels had very dull jobs. Together with hundreds of other women, they were given a hammer with which they had to take apart batteries and then separate the rod and the lignite inside. Lignite, or brown coal, made you terribly dirty and it also made you cough.

Dull as life was in Westerbork, Anne also managed to see its positive sides. She could go outside, finally talk to others,

move about. The food wasn't great, but it hadn't been great in the Annexe for a long time either. They got dirty, but were able to chat during the work. And when they had finished they could take a shower and see Father, Peter and the other men. The mattress of straw wasn't comfortable, but the thought of Mother and Margot nearby made up for that.

Still, fear remained that they would be transported. Other prisoners had told them that until recently, a train had left for Eastern Europe every week. These weekly transports seemed to have stopped. But this could be temporary. If a train left it would always be on a Tuesday. The shed leaders would announce the names of people that were on the list for a transport to the east on Monday evenings. The prisoners were not exactly sure what happened there, but they didn't trust it. If it was only to work, why were sick people transported? And young mothers with babies? And young children and the elderly? Anne thought about what they'd heard on the radio at the Annexe during the broadcasts from England. They told the others about the killings in the east.

'But surely we don't have to leave, Pim?'

Father didn't respond. What could he say? He didn't know.

Almost four weeks and three Tuesdays had passed. No trains had left the camp. There were rumours that the Allied Forces were winning. It wouldn't be long now. The war would be over soon. Perhaps the Nazis would now totally cease sending people to the East. After all, the Russian troops were beating them on that side.

'How do you think Mr Kugler and Mr Kleiman are doing?' Anne asked Peter one night. They were quietly talking behind the barbed wire. 'What would the Nazis have done to them? And to Miep and Bep? I often wonder and think of them. What about you?'

Peter nodded his head. 'I hope we will be able to thank them for all their help after the war.'

'After the war,' Anne repeated. *After the war*. Those words were unbelievably beautiful.

Then, completely out of the blue, on the evening of Saturday 2 September 1944, the shed management made an announcement. There would be another transport. Not on Tuesday, as per usual, but the next day, on Sunday. That evening, Father, Mother, Anne and Margot held hands tightly when the list was read out.

Letter A. Crying.

Letter B. Someone fainted.

Letter C. Silence.

Letter D. Two people hugged each other.

Letter E. One more to go.

Letter F. Please God, don't let it be us.

'Franco, Manfred,' the shed leader read.

A nervous wreck, hot and cold at the same time.

'Frank...'

Indescribable panic.

'...Arthur.'

A sigh of relief.

'Frank, Isaac.'

This was too difficult, too hard.

'Frank,' – don't let it be true! – 'Margot.'

Mother dropped her head.

'Frank, Otto.'

Father embraced both his daughters.

'Frank-Holländer, Edith.'

Anne's heart jumped in her throat.

'Frank, Anneliese.'

Horror

During World War II a total of 107,000 Jewish people were transported from Westerbork. These people were brought by train to camps in Eastern Europe. Usually they did not know where they would end up and what would await them. Even in their worst nightmares they could not have imagined the things that would take place there. Only 5,000 of these 107,000 Jews survived these camps.

Anne, her family and the other people who had hidden in the Annexe were also transported. They were all on the last train that would ever leave Westerbork for Auschwitz. In this concentration camp, situated in German-occupied Poland, more than a million people were murdered during World War II.

Anne and Margot were separated from their parents after a few months and were taken to Bergen-Belsen, a camp in Germany. A few survivors, among them Anne's friend Hanneli, met Anne in either Westerbork, Auschwitz or Bergen-Belsen. The few things we know about Anne's life in the last few months, we know because of their sad accounts.

Even in their worst nightmares they could not have imagined the things that would take place in the camps.

Anne's death

Anne looked at the small pile of clothes and personal belongings on her bed. She had handed them in on their arrival at Westerbork. Now that they were leaving, they had been returned to her. She removed her blue overalls, stepped out of her clogs and put them on a pile on the floor. For the first time in a month she put on her own clothes and shoes. Apart from her cropped hair, she almost looked like her old self again. On this horrible day.

The eight people in hiding had all been scheduled for the transport. They were part of a long line that was brought to the platform early that morning. The train was ready. How many people were here? A thousand perhaps. Men, women, children, old people, sick people. Everywhere men stood armed with lists and guns. They ticked off names and directed people to the appropriate wagon.

Anne, Margot and their parents were also sent to a train wagon. This time it wasn't a regular passenger train, but one for transporting animals or goods. There were no seats or toilets. The floor was covered with straw. There were two buckets, one empty and one filled with water. Next to the

bucket with water was a mug. A can with a candle was
attached to the ceiling. And that was all. There were no
windows. Two small shutters at the top of the wagon would
let in some fresh air and some light. Only those tall enough
and standing close to them would be able to look outside.
One after another they got in. Ten, twenty, fifty, sixty,
perhaps as many as seventy people. It was impossible for all of
them to sit down. Standing room only for most and taking
turns in sitting down.

The wooden sliding door slammed shut. The wagon was
dark apart from the little slivers of light coming through the
shutters. They heard the door being bolted from the outside
with a heavy bar. A high-pitched whistle. Slowly the train
began to move.

'How long will this trip last, Dad?' Anne asked.

But Father could not answer that question. Perhaps a day.
Maybe two. Would the Allied Forces be nearby and in time
to liberate them? At Westerbork the food had been bad and
work had been hard. Still, they had not been shouted at, or
beaten and kicked. It had been cruel, but bearable. The new

camp mightn't be that bad either, and liberation could be around the corner. Don't give up hope now!

Anyone who had to go to the toilet had to make do with that one bucket. Anyone who was thirsty chose the other. But the longer the journey went on, the fuller the toilet bucket would become, while the other one became empty. Their legs became tired. And they were hungry. The journey seemed to go on forever. Would this train ever stop?

'I'm so tired, Mummy,' Anne said.

'Lean on me, sweetheart.'

Another day passed. Faeces now lay next to the bucket and urine flowed freely over the floor of the wagon. The stench and sharp smell of sweat made everyone nauseous. Small children cried incessantly.

'It cannot be much further, surely?' Anne said.

But nobody knew. Again evening came. The little food they had been able to bring had long since gone. Thirst. They were all so, so thirsty.

'Oh my God,' they heard from the other side of the wagon. A man had collapsed. 'I think he is dead,' a young woman said and she burst into tears. How much worse could this nightmare get? And the train rolled on, and on. Where in heaven's name were they going? Why did they not get any food, any water or fresh air? They were being treated like cattle. What? Like cattle? No, worse than cattle. Brutal. That's what it was!

Father cuddled Anne and wrapped an arm around Margot. Mother stroked their cropped hair. 'Hang in there!' they whispered to each other. 'Don't give up!' But they were intensely tired and hungry. How long had they been travelling for? Two days? Three?

It had been dark outside for a while when they felt the train suddenly brake and slowly come to a halt. A bright light shone through the shutters. They heard dogs barking and men shouting. Then they heard the iron bolt sliding away. The wooden sliding door opened. An enormous floodlight shone into the wagon. Men dressed in blue-white striped outfits and armed with clubs urged the people from the train onto the platform. 'Hurry up!' they shouted in German. 'Faster!'

Through speakers they heard an announcement which ordered them to leave their luggage behind and line up in groups: men with men, women with women. Nobody spoke,

there were shouts and orders. People cried and shouted in fear when forced to let go of a loved one. Anne, Margot and Mother looked at Father in shock, but he whispered: 'Be brave. Keep faith.' There was no time for goodbyes, no time for a hug. They would see each other in a while. Surely. But there wasn't even time to think. There was no room for thought. All the images on the platform, the light, the dogs, the guns and clubs, were so frightening that it numbed all thoughts. Father went one way, they were ushered the other. Mother held Anne tightly with one hand and Margot with the other. *Stay together! Don't let go!* They were lined up with women and children. 'Auschwitz,' a woman whispered quietly to nobody in particular. She sounded defeated. 'This is Auschwitz.'

'For children under the age of fifteen, for the sick and elderly trucks are located at the end of the platform!' the speakers announced.

'Don't go,' a man in a blue-white striped outfit whispered. The man spoke in Dutch. How was that possible? Were these men prisoners too? But why were they carrying clubs? And why did the man warn them?

Half of all people that had arrived by train walked towards the trucks. Some were ordered to stand to the side. Dogs barked. Mother, Margot and Anne were almost at the front of the queue. They saw a man in military uniform wearing high, shiny boots. He didn't say anything. He just made tiny gestures with his hand. Sometimes to the left, other times to the right. It was their turn. Margot. To that side. Mother. The same. Anne. The same side too. Where was Father? They couldn't see him anymore.

They later heard that this had been the moment of life or

death. Those who had been sent to the other side were killed that same day. They had been deemed unfit for work by the Nazis. The same fate had awaited all those who were taken to the trucks.

'WALK!' the guards and the men in the blue-white striped outfits shouted. Those who didn't hurry were beaten with clubs. The women and girls over fifteen walked in a long line through the night. It was hard to keep up.

'WALK!'

Why was everyone so horribly mean?

'WALK!'

They saw wooden sheds and brick buildings. Further down they saw a large flame and thick black smoke. Probably a chimney, but it was hard to make out in the darkness.

A strange, putrid smell lingered in the air. A smell foreign to them all. Barbed wire was everywhere, so much barbed wire. It was quiet. Apart from the guards, they couldn't see anybody. It was night.

Again they had to line up.

'WAIT!'

There they were. Reeling on their legs. Waiting and waiting. While the first light of dawn appeared, they could slowly make out the amount of grey sheds and buildings of the camp. All sheds were built in orderly rows. The railway line crossed the centre. And far away indeed a chimney went up in the sky, still emanating black smoke.

'WALK!'

After hours of standing, they now had to follow the guards to a large stone building. There they had to say the first letter of their surname and those with 'A' were made to go in first. All other letters followed.

Inside, paperwork was done first. And once that was finished a guard would bark: 'Get undressed! Take everything off!' Everything. Hand in clothes. No loitering!

A row of women was sitting down and Anne was sent to one of them. She had to hold out her left arm. The woman marked the inside of her left forearm with a pen with a very sharp tip; the letter 'A' followed by a number. Mother and Margot also received an 'A' with a number. Then they continued to another row of women. These women were carrying scissors and razor blades. Hair had to go. All hair. Everywhere. Then they were made to stand again. And wait. Naked, bald and dizzy with tiredness, hunger and thirst. Guards with dogs were walking around.

They were allowed a short shower, but there wasn't any soap. The water was either boiling hot or freezing cold. They were each thrown one piece of clothing. Just like that. Size didn't matter. There were no towels. You were assigned two

shoes. Or sandals. Or clogs. Size 6 or 3. Or one of each. One left and one right shoe. Or two right shoes. You had to take it as it came. You were a prisoner after all.

Eventually Anne, Margot and Mother were taken to a shed. Apart from some wooden benches, it was filled mainly with wooden scaffolding three stories high with thin straw mattresses. Bunk beds apparently. One such 'bed' would sometimes sleep up to eight women. Here, hundreds of women lived. Well, live. Survive, perhaps. Or not.

That night Anne cuddled up close to Mother and Margot, as she would do every night from then on while they were together at the camp. They would make it. They would support each other through this. 'Keep going!' Mother would say repeatedly. 'Keep going!' And Anne promised herself to do just that. The Nazis would not get her down. Oh no. There were rumours the Russians were approaching. They would surely liberate them!

Thus the first weeks in Auschwitz passed. They barely had food or drink. The little they had, made them feel ill. Stomach aches made them go to those terribly filthy toilets. Whole days were spent hungry and thirsty, and working to the bone. Sometimes digging fields, other times carrying stones, with no apparent goal.

'Get up! Fast! Roll call!'

When Anne first heard this, she did not know what to do.

'Mum?' she asked.

'Do as they say,' Mother said. 'Walk tall!'

She grabbed Margot and Anne's hands and walked outside. All women from the shed had to line up in rows of five making up five lines. Standing in groups of twenty five made it easier for the guards to count them quickly.

Sometimes, though, they made the women stand like this for hours. Even on cold days. Even when all they wore was a summer dress. Or were barefoot. Or when they hadn't eaten or drunk anything.

Women who fell ill or were weak were singled out by Nazi doctors. They had to go away and were never seen again. Everyone feared having to go with them one day. They knew these women would be killed by the Nazis in gas chambers, large rooms that were filled with gas from the ceiling. Bodies were burned afterwards in the large ovens. That's what they had seen on first arrival when the black smoke had come out of the chimneys, the chimneys at the end of the railway track. And if they, the women, didn't do exactly as they were told by the guards, that's where they would end up too.

'Why are they killing Jewish men, women and children?' Anne asked Mother. But Mother did not have any answers. This evil was incomprehensible.

One morning Anne was shocked to discover her body was covered in spots. Itchy spots. Seeing this, Mother's shock was even greater. 'Try to cover it as much as possible!' she said worriedly. 'Don't show anybody and, whatever you do, keep on working.' She gave Anne a meaningful look. Anne

understood. But the spots wouldn't go away. They worsened, and became bad enough for Anne to even have to go to the hospital shed.

'I'm going with Anne,' Margot said. 'I'm not letting her go on her own.'

Mother stayed outside the hospital shed. Perhaps she could find something to eat for her girls there too.

As there were no medications available, going to the hospital shed did not improve Anne's situation. The fear of being selected by the Nazi doctors and being sent to the gas chambers, as happened to so many of the sick, was almost unbearable. But this didn't happen. Anne, Margot and Mother became weaker every day, but they lived.

At the end of October 1944 something happened that Mother, Anne and Margot had feared all this time. Together with hundreds of other women, Anne and Margot, as well as Mrs Van Pels, were selected to go to another camp. Mother had to stay. 'My children, oh my God!' she cried as both girls were taken away. She was distraught with grief.

Another train. Margot and Anne huddled together, paralysed with fear. Hungry, thirsty, filthy. Hour after hour on the train. Day after day. Sometimes crying and dispirited. Sometimes with no feelings left whatsoever. Would Father still be alive? They didn't think so. They hadn't heard from him or seen him either. And Mother? Would she be able to carry on? She was so scrawny.

Every minute took them further away from their parents. And from Peter. If he was still alive. And from Mr Pfeffer and Mr Van Pels. If they had managed to keep going at all.

They arrived in Germany, in a camp called Bergen-Belsen. There was no space for new prisoners. There were too many already. It rained. It stormed. The tents that were their temporary home collapsed in the blustery weather, so they had to find a spot in the sheds that were already filled to the rafters. There was hardly any food or drink, and if there was, it could hardly be called that. So many people died, that it became impossible to bury all the corpses. They were laid outside the sheds in piles. How could they ever find joy again?

Winter came. There was no food left. There were no warm clothes. There were no blankets.

'I'll take them off,' Anne said one day. She threw her flimsy clothes on the frozen earth.

'Don't do that, Anne,' Margot responded in horror.

'But all those bugs in my clothes,' Anne shuddered. 'They drive me crazy.'

'We all have lice and nits, Anne. Please, put on your clothes.'

But Anne refused to wear them. She now walked around with only a blanket covering her scrawny, spotted body.

'Here,' said a fellow prisoner who had done her best to find Anne some other clothes. 'Put these on, please.' Anne agreed. Fine. That's how the women tried to help each other if they could still muster the strength.

'Anne, is that really you?'

One day Anne heard a girl call her name. She came closer. Did she know her? She really needed to look carefully. But then there was recognition. 'Nanny!'

Nanny had been in Anne's class in Amsterdam. She was one of the girls that had attended her thirteenth birthday party.

'Anne,' Nanny said again as if she almost couldn't believe it was really Anne Frank in front of her. 'You're shivering.'

'I'm cold,' Anne said. 'Very cold.'

'How did you get here?'

'We were in hiding in Amsterdam. But we were betrayed.'

'Are you here by yourself?'

Anne shook her head. 'Margot is here. We are together. I've lost my parents though. What about you?'

'I'm alone.'

They stood there quietly for a moment, each with their own grief.

'What was it like being in hiding?' Nanny asked.

'I wrote everything down,' Anne said. 'I want to write a book about it.'

Nanny nodded her head. Anne had always loved writing. 'Where is Margot?'

'Ill. I have to go and see to her.'

'Let's try and see each other again, shall we?' Nanny asked.

Anne smiled. It was good to see a face she knew.

But Nanny wasn't the only friend Anne met at the camp.

One day, Mrs Van Pels came over to see Anne. 'Anne, you have to come. There is someone here for you. It's Hanneli!'

Anne couldn't believe her ears. Hanneli. She had often thought her friend had died, and now she was here?

'Hanneli?' Anne walked to the wall that was erected of barbed wire and bales of straw and divided one part of the camp from the other. On the other side she heard a voice.

'Anne! How are you? I don't understand. I thought you were in Switzerland?'

But Anne told Hanneli they had been in Amsterdam in hiding at Father's office building. It had been Father's intention to let everybody think they had fled to Switzerland. She cried. 'I believe Father and Mother are dead by now. It's just Margot and me left.'

'My father, grandmother and little sister are here. But Father is ill. I'm looking after my little sister.' Hanneli cried too.

Hanneli was staying in a part of the camp that was looked after a bit better than the part Anne was in and she tried to gather some food for her friend and throw it over the wall. This didn't work the first time as someone else caught it and fled, but the second time Anne was able to get it. They spoke briefly, because what they were doing was strictly forbidden.

'Look after yourself, Anne.'

'You too, Hanneli. And give your little sister a big cuddle from me.'

Still, dark clouds continued to gather over the lives of Margot and Anne. Like so many prisoners, Margot became ill. Very ill. As did Anne. They contracted typhoid, a very contagious disease spread by lice. They had a fever and were hot one day,

while shivering with cold the next. They tried to get up, but felt dizzy from the headaches. They tried to find food. Or something to drink. But if they ever found something, they couldn't keep it in. They tried to keep each other going. Tried to encourage each other, comfort each other. But they kept getting weaker. They looked at each other, but did they still recognise one another?

Anne leaned her tiny, tired body against Margot's to try and get warm. But Margot was cold, so cold.

Anne wanted to think of all the beautiful things in life. Of the chestnut tree behind the Annexe. Of Mother's strawberry pie. Of Father telling her a wonderful story. But she could not go on anymore. She no longer felt hunger, sorrow or loneliness. She was going to sleep, to sleep long and deep. Just like Margot.

What happened next

Summer 1945. Nazi Germany was defeated. Hitler was dead. High ranking Nazis were arrested and put on trial. Dutch people tried to resume normal life. A lot of work had to be done. New houses were urgently needed, railway tracks, the bridges and the airport needed to be repaired, but above all people had to have enough to eat again.

Otto Frank returned to The Netherlands after a long trip home. During this journey he already found out that his wife had died in Auschwitz. He hoped to find Anne and Margot alive. Back in Amsterdam, however, a survivor told him about the deaths of his daughters in Bergen-Belsen. Otto was the only one of the eight people in hiding to survive. Herman and Auguste van Pels, as well as their son Peter, had not survived the Nazi's cruelties. Fritz Pfeffer was murdered too. The helpers, however, had all survived the war. Again they were there to help him.

When it became apparent that Anne would not return, Miep handed Otto Anne's diary and her notebooks and notes. She and Bep had found these in the Annexe after the arrest. Miep had kept them all this time in a drawer of her desk, hoping to one day return them to Anne.

Otto read the notes piece by piece. It was a painful process. But it also surprised him. What a wonderful storyteller Anne had been! How meticulously had she written about their time in the Annexe. So full of wisdom. So full of deep thoughts. He also read about her wish to become a writer and publish a book for which she had even thought of a title: *The Secret Annexe*.

'But, and that's the big question, will I ever be able to write something great will I ever become a journalist or a writer?' Anne wrote a year before her death. Otto was in no doubt. Anne was a writer. Although Anne had died, her voice emanated loud and clear from the pages of her diary. From then on Otto only had one goal: to fulfil his daughter's dream. He would make sure *The Secret Annexe* would be published.

Family album

Otto Frank was a keen amateur photographer. Through the
years he photographed Anne and Margot many times. These
pictures have survived. He was unable to continue this
hobby while in hiding. The last photo he took of Anne dates
from just before going into hiding. At that point Anne was
13 years of age.

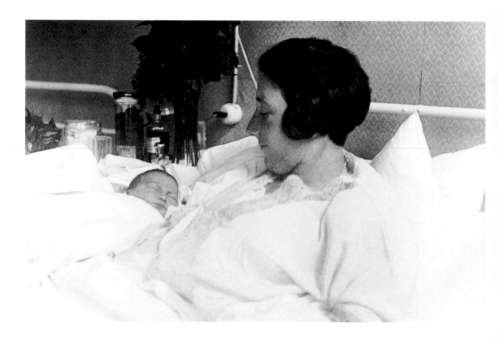

Baby Anne, just one day old, and her mother, 13 June 1929.

Baby Anne on the balcony, 1930. Behind her Margot and girl next door Gertrud Naumann. Gertrud would often babysit Anne and Margot.

Anne and Margot with their father, August 1931.

On a hot day Margot gets showered by Grace,
who lived next door. Anne curiously looks on (1932).

Anne and Margot with their mother in the city centre of Frankfurt am Main, March 1933. By then, Anne's parents had decided to move to The Netherlands.

Anne in kindergarten, Amsterdam 1934.

Anne with her friend Sanne on Merwede Square, 1935. Sanne plays with a hoop, Anne with a skipping rope.

Anne (right) with her friends Sanne (centre) and Eva on
Merwede Square, Amsterdam, July 1936.

Anne and her friends in the sandbox, July 1937. From left to
right: Hanneli Goslar, Anne, Dolly Citroen, Hannah Toby,
Barbara and Sanne Ledermann.

Anne feeds a pet rabbit, June 1938.

Anne's tenth birthday, 12 June 1939. From left to right: Lucie van Dijk, Anne, Sanne Ledermann, Hanneli Goslar, Juultje Ketellapper, Käthe Egyedie, Mary Bos, Ietje Swillens, Martha van den Berg.

Anne with Dopy in the village of Laren, 1940. Dopy was owned by her parents' friends.

Anne with her parents and sister,
Merwede Square, May 1941.

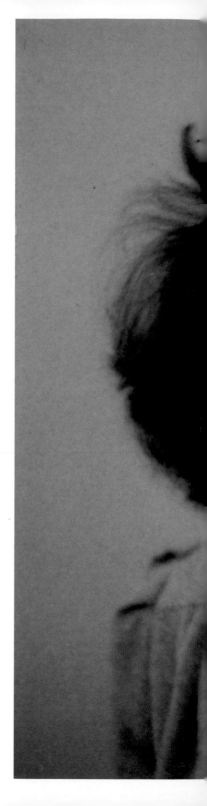

Anne shortly before her thirteenth
birthday, May 1942. This is the last
known picture that was taken of
her. Two months later she had to
go into hiding.

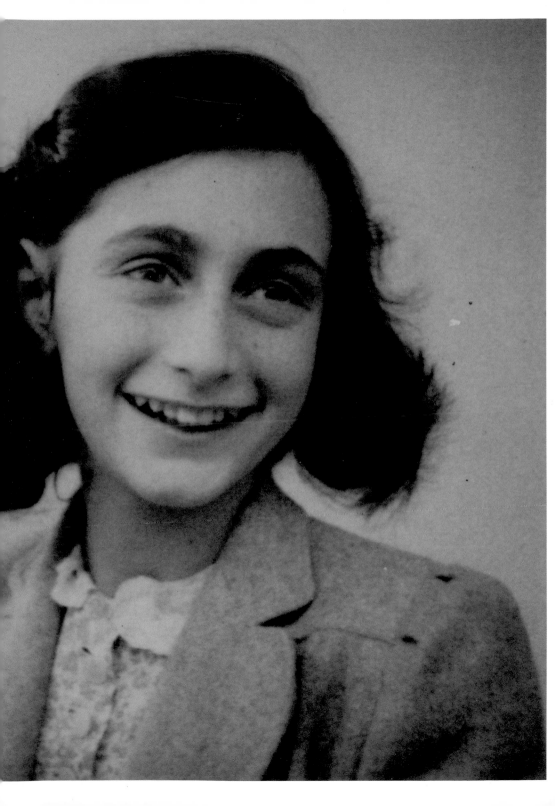

Anne's father Otto with the helpers after the War, October 1945. From left to right: Miep Gies, Johannes Kleiman, Otto Frank, Victor Kugler and Bep Voskuijl.

Accountability

Wherever possible, the stories in this book are based on historical events and sources; notes and stories from Anne herself, from her father, the helpers and other people who knew Anne and her family. To understand the story of Anne Frank and make it accessible for children, we sometimes made up conversations she might have had. But these too are based on known sources and were intended to stay as close as possible to events as they had happened.

Books

Anne Frank, *The Diary of a Young Girl*. Puffin Books (Penguin Group), 2007

Anne Frank, *Tales from the Secret Annex*. US edition published by Bantam Dell, 2003

Jacqueline van Maarsen, *My name is Anne, she said, Anne Frank*. Arcadia Books, 2008

Jacqueline van Maarsen, *Je beste vriendin Anne*. Querido 2011 (not available in English)

Alison Leslie Gold, *Hannah Goslar remembers: a childhood friend of Anne Frank*. Bloomsbury, 1998

The NIOD Institute for War, Holocaust and Genocide Studies, *The Diary of Anne Frank: The Critical Edition*. US edition published by Doubleday, 1989

Quotes

The quotes in *Outside it's War* refer to the following passages in the diary of Anne Frank.
Anne Frank, the Diary of a Young Girl – Puffin Books (Penguin Group) 2007. Edited by Otto H. Frank and Mirjam Pressler; translated by Susan Massotty.

Page 73: '(..)vests,(..), a dress, (..) a skirt, a jacket (..)' Wednesday, 8 July 1942

Page 91: The best little table – Tuesday, 13 July 1943

Page 91: Shamefully self-centred – Tuesday, 13 July 1943

Page 95: 'I keep seeing her enormous eyes, and they haunt me.' Saturday, 27 November 1943

Page 97: 'Footsteps in the house, the private office, the kitchen, then... on the staircase. All sounds of breathing stopped, eight hearts pounded. Footsteps on the stairs, then a rattling at the bookcase.' Tuesday, 11 April 1944

Page 100-101: 'Writing in a diary is a really strange experience for someone like me. Not only because I've never written anything before, but also because it seems to me that later on neither I nor anyone else will be interested in the musings of a thirteen-year-old schoolgirl.' Saturday, 20 June 1942

Page 103: 'They certainly sound beautiful, but they mean very little to me.' Thursday, 29 October 1942

Page 107-108: 'Once upon a time there were two people, and old woman and her granddaughter, who lived for many years at the edge of a great big forest.'
'She lay down on her bed and wept'.

'You mustn't think that I'll stop looking after you now that I'm dead. I'm in Heaven, watching you from up above.'
Tales from the Secret Annex by Anne Frank
Book of short stories and events from the Annex.
Story: The Guardian Angel
US edition published by Bantam Dell, 2003
Edited by Gerrold van der Stroom and Susan Massotty
Translated by Susan Massotty

Front house | Annexe

1 Store room
2 Office kitchen
3 Private office
4 Victor Kugler's office
5 Miep Gies, Johannes Kleiman and
  Bep Voskuijl's office
6 Warehouse
7 Front house attic
8 The bookcase

9 Otto, Edith and Margot Frank's room
10 Anne Frank and Fritz Pfeffer's room
11 Washroom
12 Hermann and Auguste van Pels's room
13 Peter van Pels's room
14 Annexe attic